ALWAYS
LOVED

BRENT LOKKER

Scripture taken from the NEW AMERICAN STANDARD BIBLE® (NASB), Copyright © 1960, 1962, 1963, 1968, 1971, 1972, 1973, 1975, 1977, 1995 by The Lockman Foundation. Used by permission. Scripture taken from the New King James Version (NJKV). Copyright © 1982 by Thomas Nelson, Inc. Used by permission. All rights reserved. Scripture taken from The Message (MSG). Copyright © 1993, 1994, 1995, 1996, 2000, 2001, 2002. Used by permission of NavPress Publishing Group. THE HOLY BIBLE, NEW INTERNATIONAL VERSION®, NIV® Copyright © 1973, 1978, 1984, 2011 by Biblica, Inc.™ Used by permission. All rights reserved worldwide. Scripture taken from The Mirror Translation (TMT) by François du Toit. www.mirrorword.net. Used by permission. Scripture taken from The New Jerusalem Bible (NJB), copyright © 1985 by Darton, Longman & Todd, Ltd. and Doubleday, a division of Random House, Inc. Reprinted by Permission. Scripture taken from The Revised Standard Version (RSV) of the Bible copyright © 1946, 1952 and 1971 by the Division of Christian Education of the National Council of Churches in the USA. Used by permission. All Rights Reserved. Scripture taken from The New Revised Standard Version of the Bible (NRSV) copyright © 1989 by the Division of Christian Education of the National Council of Churches in the USA. Used by permission. All Rights Reserved. Scripture taken from the Contemporary English Version (CEV) © American Bible Society 1991, 1992, 1995. Used with permission. Scripture taken from The Bible in Basic English (BBE), which is in the public domain. Scripture taken from The Source New Testament (TSNT). Copyright © 2004 by Ann Nyland. Used by permission of Smith and Stirling Publishing. All rights reserved. Scripture taken from The Bible: James Moffatt Translation (JMT), Copyright © 1922, 1924, 1925, 1926, 1935 Harper Collins, San Francisco, CA, Copyright © 1950, 1952, 1953, 1954. Scripture taken from The New Testament: A Translation by William Barclay. Westminster John Knox Press. © The Estate of William Barclay, 1968, 1999. Scripture taken from The Word on the Street. Published by Zondervan. Copyright © 2003,2004 by Rob Lacey. Scripture taken from the Common English Bible®, CEB® Copyright © 2010, 2011 by Common English Bible.™ Used by permission. All rights reserved worldwide.

Cover design: Yvonne Parks of www.pearcreative.ca
Interior: David Sluka at www.david-sluka.com

**ALWAYS LOVED
YOU ARE HIS TREASURE, NOT HIS PROJECT**

Paperback ISBN-13: 978-0-9882164-2-6
ebook ISBN-13: 978-0-9882164-3-3

Contact Brent Lokker at www.brentlokkerministries.com

Printed in the United States of America

Endorsements

The purpose of *Always Loved* can be summed up in this verse: *"We love, because He first loved us"* (1 John 4:19). Discovering the love that is beyond measure has been a great challenge for so many. Author Brent Lokker does all of us a great service by addressing the lies that hinder our perception of such love and the truths that supersede such lies. Chapter by chapter, you will journey into the full discovery of His love that doesn't have to be earned. You will be encouraged by realizing who you are in the Father's eyes, which then makes it normal to truly love the broken and to carry out great exploits.

BILL JOHNSON

Author of *Hosting the Presence* and *When Heaven Invades Earth*

I just experienced waves of liquid love as I read this book. The Agape Reformation has started. Brent is a lover who will take you into the affection of your Heavenly Father. The Baptism of Love is personal, powerful, and passionate. Transform your life and the world around you by receiving love and giving it away.

LEIF HETLAND

Author of *Seeing Through Heaven's Eyes*

The whole church world is being enlivened by a rediscovery of God as Father. To know Him at any level is to recognize that of all the things He wanted to be called, Jesus who knows His Father's heart, commanded us to pray, "Our Father . . . " Had He wanted something besides sons and daughters, He would have had us call Him something besides a Father! The rediscovery of God as Father is at the heart of revival and as the truth and dynamic of is known, the fruit of this reviving will prove immediate and residual.

The Father/Son paradigm is not only the centerpiece of civilization; it is the DNA of the entire cosmos. Thank you, Brent, for a clear voice and a good read in this splendid book.

JACK TAYLOR

President, Dimensions Ministries, Melbourne FL

At the high price of the Cross of Christ, the Lord of the Universe birthed sons and daughters. In *Always Loved* Brent invites you to personally encounter what Jesus paid for: the pure love, pleasure and acceptance of our Heavenly Father.

Each chapter beckons you to enjoy the privileged relationship that you are meant to experience as Abba's beloved child—you will find yourself living, thinking and believing as a son or daughter and bringing Heaven to Earth as you walk into the full riches of your divine inheritance.

GEORGIAN BANOV
President and Co-Founder of Global Celebration

This book comes from the heart-fought struggle of a servant realizing he is a beloved son. Watching this amazing metamorphosis gives Brent all the credibility he needs to write a book in leading others to freedom, joy and peace. Get ready to break free from the performance trap as you experience this book.

DANNY SILK
Author of *The Culture of Honor*

What Jesus reveals about the Father of the human race puts the devil and religion out of business! *Have we not all one father? Has not one God created us?* (Malachi 2:10) In God we discover that we are not here by chance or accident, or by the desire of an earthly parent. Neither are we the product of a mere physical conception. We exist by the expression of God's desire to reveal Himself in the flesh.

Thank you Brent Lokker for your bold declaration of the Father! This is a most needed message that the world must hear!

FRANCOIS DU TOIT
Author of *The Mirror Translation*

There are good messages, there are significant thoughts, and then there are strategic holy summons that carry a fiery mandate meant to revolutionize the masses. I make it a point to wake up each morning and intentionally receive the inward affirmation and adoration of the Father. I'm convinced that this might be one of the most significant catalysts on the earth. Jesus embodies the perfect model and will of the Father for all of His sons and daughters and He began His ministry with this epic Paternal download. The Old Testament concludes with this mandate that centers around turning the hearts of the fathers to the hearts of the sons or else a curse is left in its wake. One of the greatest disorders (curses) in our hour is the orphaned spirit that drives so many towards an illegitimate mentality and lifestyle. Yet, in order for us to fully walk in this coming move of God (which will sweep the earth and bring about a massive harvest), we must get this message deep down in our hearts.

Brent has written a profound, heartfelt and revelatory book on what is the primary locomotive of the Kingdom—the Father's Affirmation and Affection. As I read portions of this book, I felt challenged to go deeper in God's love and I also felt healing from it's Truth. It's been said, "There are few things more powerful than an idea whose time has come." *Always Loved* is an idea that is both timeless and very NOW! Some messages tweak you and other messages transform you! Revival is coming to the earth in greater dimensions and this TRUTH will be one of the catalysts for the greatest number of exploits and people brought into the Kingdom...ever!

SEAN SMITH

Author of *Prophetic Evangelism* and *I Am Your Sign*

www.seansmithminstries.com

@revseansmith

I never get bored with the message of the Father's Love but I especially love to hear it from those that live it well. Brent is a habitual receiver and giver of the Love of God and was, long before he thought of writing a book. It is this posture of being a lover which has caused him to write in a way which encourages not mere understanding but experience of the love of God towards us. In fact he dares us to believe it is true.

My own journey of learning to receive the Father's love has radically changed every area of my life as it has countless others. Perhaps this is your first encounter of this teaching, in which case it will change your life too, or perhaps you are familiar with the message in which case I encourage you to open your heart to the more which is about to be revealed.

Though increasingly a common subject this message is not to be treated lightly! Assumed familiarity is a danger which can prevent us from receiving what God "our Daddy" has for us. It cannot merely be learned it must be encountered and this book will lead you through Brent's personal experiences, stories and teaching to encounter after encounter.

As for me I continue to learn from every angle taken to teach about being loved and loving our heavenly Dad. Whatever your role in life get ready for an upgrade. This last year I was pursued by this message and discovered how essential it is in an area which I am gifted: 'The Gift of Administration', learning that managing and leading must come from the heart of a son. This book will lead you on your own journey and as with my particular ministry it will bring an upgrade to yours as you embrace the heart of a son or daughter.

PAUL MANWARING
Author of What On Earth Is Glory and Kisses From a Good God

Wow! *Always Loved* is an amazing book of connecting with God's Father heart for us all. Born out of real life experiences, Brent Lokker speaks with authority in this area. It will bring healing and lift you to unlimited possibilities through God's love.

DOUG ADDISON
InLight Connection, Author of *Understand Your Dreams Now*
www.dougaddison.com

In his book, *Always Loved*, Brent Lokker strikes at the heart of the enemy's strategy to leave God's people feeling fatherless and without value. As you read this book you cannot help but be overwhelmed with the immense goodness of the Father and His wholehearted commitment to claim you as His own.

Brent's message is an authentic expression of his personal journey and intimate relationship with the Father. His powerful revelations lead the reader beyond learning and into an encounter with the transforming love of God. This book is a journey into a life-giving embrace.

DAVID CRONE
Senior Leader of The Mission in Vacaville, CA and
Author of The Power of Your Life Message and Decisions that Define Us

There's always passion whenever you're talking about your life message, and that's what comes across in Brent's book *Always Loved*. And this is such a needed message. A recent national survey showed that 78% of Americans have a distorted view of God, seeing God as authoritative, controlling, critical or distant. Only 22 percent of those surveyed saw Him as a loving, benevolent God. And we're certain those statistics aren't limited to just the USA—it's universal.

This is a timely message that shines through not only Brent's book, but also in the church that he and his wife, Suzanne, pastor. Father God is wildly, madly, passionately in love with His children, and when we take hold of that message, we can become His agents of love here on planet earth. Through the pages of this book, Brent take us on a journey to discover the true heartbeat of Father God toward us, changing our mindsets, and drawing us into actually experiencing His love for us. And, as Brent points out through wonderful stories, it's a love that can cause us to change the culture around us.

We've been privileged to minister numerous times at Blazing Fire and can testify, this book was born out of Brent and his church *actually* living out this life message—a message of the Father's love. We heartily recommend this book to you.

BILL & CAROL DEW
Revivalists, Founders of Dewnamis Ministries
and Authors of *Living the Miraculous Life*

As a great apostolic movement sweeps the earth, experiencing the Father's love is still the great heartbeat and core petition of this movement. Historically, knowing and experiencing the love of the Father was the epicenter of the Apostle Paul's prayers. In, *Always Loved*, Brent Lokker not only hits ground zero in the heart of the Father but exposes his own heart journey as well. This book delivers the blessings that break off your performance shackles and help you step in to the boundless affection of your Heavenly Father.

DAN MCCOLLAM
Sounds of the Nations, Global Legacy Apostolic Team
The Mission in Vacaville, CA

There is no shortage in the world of negativity, judgment, brokenness, bad news, or the celebration of someone else's demise. Is it any wonder people don't know how to receive, accept, or embrace the love of God? Where are the examples of God's love? In *Always Loved,* Brent Lokker takes us on a journey of intimate discovery where we don't just "hear" God loves us, but one where we encounter personally the love of God, our Father. Who can encounter, yet not receive, the tender gaze, warm embrace, and peaceful, safe, tangible feeling of God's love? If you've searched the world over for love and been left with a feeling of "there's got to be more," you've found the best path to discovering, encountering, and living in God's love through this marvelous work of Brent's. Once freely received, love can be freely given to a dying, hurting, lost world stripped bare of love. As you turn the pages of *Always Loved,* you are one step... one moment closer to walking in the liberating love of your creator and sharing that love with the world around you.

DICK BERNAL
Senior Pastor of Jubilee Christian Center, San Jose, CA
Author of *Shaking Hands with God*

Brent is a gift to the San Francisco Bay Area and the body of Christ. Everyone who has the joy of meeting him has been brushed by the love that he writes about in this book.

This book is a bridge that will help you cross from knowing the truth of God's love and affection to actually experiencing and expressing it. The discovery revealed here has the power to forever transform whoever receives it. Prepare for an encounter with your Abba!

CALEB & RACHEL KLINGE
Lead Pastors of New Life Christian Center in Novato, CA

Without a doubt, Brent Lokker has been profoundly touched by Father God's amazing love. As you read *Always Loved,* His amazing love for you will become more evident with each page you turn. Daddy's heartbeat will become the rhythm of the "life of love" that increasingly defines your journey!

GAYLORD ENNS
Author of *Love Revolution: Rediscovering the Lost Command of Jesus*

Pastor Brent Lokker has done us a great favor writing *Always Loved.* This book is a thoughtful, balanced and yet impassioned view of God's love for us, His 21st Century Bride. Many people can experience frustration when in the midst of renewal. Relationship with Father, for whatever reason, seems to slip away. The message of this book is a missing ingredient that will help many understand and rest in Daddy's Love! Thanks Brent for reminding us that HIS LOVE FOR US saturates everything!"

RICHARD OLIVER

Pastor and Overseer of The River, International Revival Network

I'm excited about Brent Lokker's book, *Always Loved*. It's God's time like no other for this message to be shared anew. I've known Brent for years now to be a man on fire and passionately in love with Jesus. Brent has exemplified our Heavenly Father's love with his kind and gracious manner and one can't help but to feel accepted and at ease when you are with him. However, recently I sensed that there was something fresh and more deeply activated in Brent that I understood better when I read some of the chapters of *Always Loved*. Brent has peeled back some layers of misconception that has hidden some precious eternal truths concerning God's grace and His extravagant love for you and me. As you read through the pages of *Always Loved*, you will be encouraged, touched, transformed. You'll discover, as Brent has, our Heavenly Father really wants you and is celebrating you right now!

PAT CHEN

President, First Love Ministries International Prayer Center, San Ramon, CA
"The Secret Place" prayer room, Washington, DC near the White House
International speaker and author of
Intimacy With the Beloved and *The Depths of God*

This book carries ESSENTIAL JOY! Your heart's happiness is richly revealed within these pages! The thrilling saga of the Covenant Love in which your life has been interwoven ... the lavish grace of never-wasted love ... all here, in beautiful, poetic prophetic prose: Your Love Story. Gospel. Very Good News!

Brent Lokker's lovely, lush writing captivates, sparkling with interior energy. His profoundly encouraging words of experienced pastoral wisdom teach you to soar. Glorious, gorgeous Grace energizes your faith as you comprehend your identity ... perhaps for the first time.

The excitement builds! As you read this easy-to-read, easy-to-understand book, you are mentored by God Your Father Himself and beautifully empowered by the Holy Spirit to understand Christ's perfect Finished Work on the Cross – all He has accomplished for you!

Most of all, here for you is Brent Lokker's life message. In these pages, The Blessing of your Heavenly Father is abundantly ministered to you in stellar beauty by a highly honored and greatly loved Father in Revival – my very dear friend Brent Lokker.

Reading this brilliantly insightful, down-to-earth book is rewarding and inspiring. I couldn't put it down … yet at the same time, I loved putting it down from time to time just to enter into a heavenly reverie inspired by the practicality of Grace (Himself). I recommend this book to all who are longing for closeness to God. Have fun!!

REV. LANI LANGLAIS
San Francisco, California USA

Contents

❧

SECTION ONE
Revealing the Tender Heart of the Father for You
He's Much Kinder than You Know

SECTION TWO
Daring to Believe It's True
Choosing to Embark Upon the Journey of a Lifetime

SECTION THREE
Living a Life of Love that Matters
Transforming Your World

Acknowledgements

My astoundingly good heavenly Father, who has done all things to set me free in Christ so I can thoroughly enjoy my unchanging status as His highly favored, beloved son!

My beautiful wife, Suzanne, who has unwaveringly believed in me and supported me every step of the way in our journey together. I'm blessed beyond measure, my Love!

My two awesome sons, Derek and Aaron, who have provided more joy to me than you'll ever know. Because of you two, I know the extreme nature of Papa God's love in a way I never could have.

The elders and all my family at Blazing Fire Church who have lived out with Suzanne and me a culture of extreme love, grace, and honor. What an amazing ride it's been thus far. The best is yet to come!

Bill Johnson and Kris Vallotton of Bethel Church in Redding, California, for being spiritual fathers to me over the past twelve years, giving me permission to be great and giving me the two thumbs up. I am so very thankful for both of you!

My dad (who's with Jesus now) and my mom, who gave me the greatest gift imaginable—a deep foundation of love, acceptance, and approval. You're the best!

Special thanks to Lisa-Anne Wooldridge and Reverend Lani Langlais, who lovingly waded through my manuscripts to make this a much better read. You two rock!

Foreword
by Kris Vallotton

The world is full of walking wounded people who long for intimacy but fear rejection. My guess is that this is the most fatherless generation in the history of the world. Broken homes, single parents, and latchkey kids are so common in our culture that it's become a habit when you see a woman with children to ask her if she is married before you ask her what her husband does for a living. All of this has created a dynamic that has distorted our view of our heavenly Father. For some people, God is like a celestial pimp who prostitutes people to get what He wants from them. But God doesn't "use people," He loves them! For others, God is like their rage-aholic stepfather who needs a place to unload some of His anger. These folks believe that God is just waiting for them to make a mistake so He can unleash hell on them. But none of these scenarios represents our heavenly Father's love for us as Brent points out so powerfully in this book.

Always Loved is more than a book; it's a Holy Spirit journey into the very heart of God Himself. Brent Lokker has done a masterful job of re-presenting the Father in a way that's both theologically sound and culturally relevant. He unmasks the lies that have polluted the minds of the multitudes, isolating them from the love and affection of the Father. Brent Lokker proves to us that God is not a cosmic control freak who tolerates His fallen creation, but a loving Daddy who celebrates His sons and daughters.

If your heart is broken and you feel rejected and abandoned, or if you simply struggle to feel loved, *Always Loved* is the book for you. It will cut a trail through the jungle of broken relationships, betrayals, and abuse, while paving a path to passion in your heart that you never thought was possible!

I highly recommend this book and believe that many people will be released from the slave camps of a loveless master into the arms of their loving Daddy.

KRIS VALLOTTON
Leader, Bethel Church, Redding, CA
Co-founder of Bethel School of Supernatural Ministry
Author of *The Supernatural Ways of Royalty* and *Spirit Wars* and others

Introduction

❧

G od is after lovers. He always has been. His heart for us will never change.

We are living in a time of increased revelation of the Father's outrageous love for His children simply because He will not rest until His true nature as a passionate lover is revealed. God will not be denied His heart's desire. That desire is closeness and intimacy with each one of us.

As we experience our heavenly Father's love and affection, no matter what we are going through, we are able to place our entire trust in the One who totally adores us. Intimacy with God is the answer to every deep heart cry that we have. Knowing and experiencing His great affection will see us victoriously through absolutely anything. I'm convinced that this is the key to living and enjoying the abundant life that Jesus promised us.

Certain individuals throughout history have grasped this true heart of the Father, but God has been eagerly anticipating an entire generation who will rise up and believe just how astoundingly good He really is. It's my conviction we are that generation, and the time is now! God has heavenly realities waiting for us that are above and beyond all we could ask or imagine. We access them by believing that His generous, extravagant heart is always for us, never against us.

I choose to be a voice to inspire a generation to leave behind, once and for all, the notion that working harder to please God will make us happier and make our lives more meaningful. Instead, the invitation and goal is simply to enjoy the One who enjoys us so much!

If you accept and receive the Father's love for you, the outcome will be a life of purpose that continually overflows and inspires those around you with that very same love. You've been invited into a place of perpetual rest in the Father's pleasure, giving you an ease to life that will lead you step by step into the fullness of your destiny with Him.

This book is written not just for you, but also for God to enjoy forever!

At first glance that statement may seem a bit presumptuous. But the reality is, we are eternal beings and what you and I do on the earth matters to God forever. Each of us has the ability to bring glory to God by displaying the unique reflection of Him that no one else can project in the exact same way. Let's all unashamedly reflect His glory in the way we were designed to shine!

For those who are seeking to know if there's a God at all, I applaud your courage to explore the possibility and I want to introduce you to a perfect Father who's been waiting your whole life to show you who He really is.

To those who view God as a distant father you can never fully please, no matter how hard you try—one who is waiting for you to make a mistake so He can unleash His punishment upon you—I have written this book to ignite hope into your hearts. I have some truly good news for you: God's heart is to bless you, not to punish you. You have some catching up to do with a Father who actually *likes* you!

I've also written this book to touch the hearts of those who feel stuck in an intellectual understanding of God's love, frustrated you can't seem to get it from your head to your heart and experience a genuine encounter of the Father's affection. For you I have exceptionally good news: God wants you to experience His affection even more than you want it, and He fully intends for you to enjoy these encounters of love with Him.

For you who are already experiencing great depths of the Father's heart, this book will be a travel guide to more fun places of exploration. In this journey with God as your Father, you need never be disappointed. Your cries for more intimacy have been clearly heard and Papa's answer is already an emphatic "YES!"

To assist you in this journey, I've included declarations of truth to agree with straight from the Father's heart to yours at the beginning of each chapter. Along the way I've provided practical suggestions to help you connect with the Lord's tenderness toward you in a more tangible way. At the end of each chapter I've included reflections to take you deeper personally or discuss with a group that may choose to go through this book together. At the end of the book I've supplied a life-giving Father's blessing for you to enjoy any time you need to be reminded of just how loved and wanted you are.

My prayer for each of you as you read this book is that you will have ever-increasing genuine encounters with your Father in heaven that lead you into deeper intimacy with Him. While reading this book, anytime the Holy Spirit touches your heart with truth that you've been longing to hear, stop and savor the moment, soaking in the goodness of God toward you. The truth sets you free, and as the Lord sets you free with His words of affirmation and acceptance, you'll see your life in a whole new way. The goal is not to rush through this book in order to check one more item off your to-do list but to enjoy, moment by moment, tender closeness with the Lord.

He's waiting for you at this very moment.

SECTION ONE

Revealing the Tender Heart of the Father for You

He's Much Kinder than You Know

Chapter 1

A Father Who Loves You with All His Heart

My child, I am your Father and you belong to Me.
Let Me draw you in and love you.
Please don't pull back from My total acceptance of you.
My love is the greatest force in the cosmos
and it's fully fixed upon YOU as My heart's true desire!

"Tell me again, Daddy!" I heard these words from my two boys when they were toddlers just after I had finished reading a story that had ushered them into a world of wonder and adventure.

Our heavenly Father loves to do the same for us, and like wide-eyed little children, each of us exclaims, "Tell me again, Daddy!"

And He is all too happy to oblige. Listen to a story from His heart: The Father's Treasure…

Once upon a time there was a Treasure that was too marvelous, too extravagant, too perfect for any earthly words to describe. Although there were treasure-hunters around the world, they were looking for earthly riches and seemed to pass right over the greatest, most costly Treasure of them all. But the Treasure never escaped My gaze. As the King and Ruler of my kingdom, I had to have it at any cost. One day, I sent My son, the Valiant Knight in Shining Armor, to seek after the Treasure and bring it back to Me. We both saw the immense worth of the Treasure and we'd both heard this living Treasure calling out to be found. With a look of intense determination and bravery, the Knight vowed to Me, "I will bring you the Treasure, My Father and King. *I must bring you the Treasure!*"

In no time at all, the Valiant Knight found the Treasure, but not without peril. For an Evil Rogue was brooding nearby, with the intent of stealing the Treasure for himself for all time to come. With one terrified glance at the Knight, the Rogue saw that his powers were no match for the supreme might of the Valiant Warrior, so he ruthlessly unsheathed his sword, turned toward the Treasure, and hissed, "If I can't have you, then no one can."

As the rage-driven sword lunged perilously toward the Treasure, the Knight leaped in and intercepted the sword right in the center of His heart. Breathing His last breath, He exclaimed, "I did it for love!" Then He crumpled lifeless to the ground.

The Dark Rogue screamed in false victory, "You fool! With your death, now and forever the Treasure is all mine!"

But suddenly and without warning, a brilliant, luminescent light flooded the Knight from within. He arched his back and sprang up from the ground to His feet with superhuman power. The sword that had pierced Him melted to nothing. With one blow of His mighty hand, the Knight smashed the Rogue to the ground and shackled him eternally in chains. Looking over the defeated, helpless villain, the

Knight exclaimed, "This Treasure is Mine and you will never, ever steal it from Me again!"

With that, the Valiant Knight in Shining Armor scooped up the Treasure and presented it to Me, the King, where it has always belonged.

The Treasure, you see, wasn't a bag of gold or a priceless painting or even the world's richest jewels. The Treasure is *YOU*, My child! You are more valuable to Me than anything and you are with Me forever, right where you belong. I have always wanted you and I will never let you go. And now I have knighted you and I have given you My eyes to see all of the Treasures that encircle the globe. You will see them as I see them, and you will tell them what a good and benevolent King I really am. And with the authority that I have given to you, you will bring them safely to Me, as befits a royal knight such as yourself.

Gazing into our heavenly Father's eyes of adoration and love, and with our mouths agape in utter amazement, we are left speechless.

Actually, there is one more phrase that passes by our lips:

"Tell me again, Daddy!"

Is it Okay to Call God "Daddy"?

You may be thinking, *Isn't it irreverent to call Yahweh, the Most Holy God, "Daddy"?* Irreverence is a failure to give proper honor, significance, or value to one who deserves it. But Jesus came to the earth to introduce the world to His misunderstood heavenly Father, giving Him all honor, significance, and value. Jesus modeled for us closeness with God that went far beyond what any of us thought we could have. He encouraged us to call God "Abba, Father!" The apostle Paul tells us the same thing—we have been given the spirit of adoption, enabling us to cry out, "Abba, Father!"[1]

> To seal our sonship, God has commissioned the Spirit of sonship to resonate the Abba echo in our hearts; and now,

in our innermost being we recognize Him as our true and
very dear Father. (Galatians 4:6 TMT)

The Hebrew word *Abba* is the most intimate, affectionate, child-
like word you could use to describe a Father. The closest English word
might be *Da-Da*.

Picture a toddler who longs to be in the fun and safe place of his
daddy's arms. So he holds up his little outstretched hands and says,
"Up, Da-Da!" What good father's heart wouldn't melt at such a tender
request from his child? Your heavenly Father's heart is melted by you!
I assure you that there is never a thought in His mind that you are being irreverent or disrespectful if you call out to Him in such childlike
sweetness. No, He gladly scoops you up into His arms and gives you
the security of His love, gazing on you with joyful affection!

However, most people experience a certain "lag time" when what
our spirit knows to be true is eventually felt with our emotions—a
seeming disconnect. One of the keys to shortening that lag time of
experiencing the truth of Daddy's great big love for you is to use your
voice. By speaking the truth out loud and hearing it audibly, you will
internalize it and own it for yourself much more readily.

I experienced this radical transformation many years ago by saying out loud a phrase that caused me to live in the certainty of God's
genuine love and affection for me. Many times a day until I believed
it to the core of my being, I would say out loud with enthusiasm and
with arms open wide to welcome His presence,

"Daddy, you love me!"

I want to encourage you to try it out *right now*. It may seem a
little awkward at first, especially if you have not known God in this
intimate way before. If you want to use a different word than Daddy
that is even more special to you, go ahead. Just be sure it's a word that
conveys tenderness to you. Say it out loud and say it like you mean it,
even if you are not feeling any warm fuzzies yet. Please set this book
down for a moment and do this.

"Daddy, you love me!"

How was that for you? For some of you, just using your voice out loud to speak this was a huge breakthrough. If you are feeling His tenderness, by all means, say it again and linger in the moment. But even if you felt nothing, don't be discouraged. Trust me that over time this will revolutionize your relationship with your heavenly Father. Keep saying this, out loud, many times a day—like you mean it—and watch what happens. If you skipped right over this exercise, now is your time to go back and say it out loud—really!

Made for Love

Every single person who has ever lived on this earth has the same basic need to be loved. We were made with an insatiable appetite for life-giving love—true, genuine love. Apart from love and nurturing acceptance, people wither and lose heart. Studies have shown that babies who are denied loving physical touch will actually die.[2]

But the need for love is not just for babies. People of all ages are dying for lack of love. For some that takes the form of an emotional death, where there is simply no more will to live even though the days on the calendar continue passing by. Attempts to numb the loneliness with all forms of excessive indulgences don't come close to easing the pain. For others it can even take the form of choosing self-destruction to try to permanently end the torment.

The Father's heart is breaking for His children. God is love, and at this very moment, He is surrounding, filling, and saturating everything and everyone He has created with His all-encompassing love.

His delight with and enjoyment of you is breaking right through any feelings of disconnectedness you may have. He is irresistibly drawing you in.

Your Father in heaven, your Papa, is crying out to you:

"I love you, My child! Hear My heart. I have *always* loved you!"

You Are Mine

I have two amazing sons, Derek and Aaron, who are now handsome young men. When each of them was born, I had the absolute thrill of a lifetime, holding them just seconds after they entered this world. Cradling each son when he was born, my emotions burst forth and I wept tears of wonder and awe. I couldn't help it! It was a miracle beyond words.

The sheer joy of tenderly securing each of my tiny, beautiful sons in my trembling hands was extremely moving. I felt so much love for my sons and I took great pleasure in them too. They were absolutely perfect! And here is a stunning truth: my sons couldn't do a single thing for me to make me love them. No, I loved them with an extreme passion and I was wildly pleased with them for one reason alone: *they were mine!* My intense feelings of massive delight for them gripped me to the core of my being as I thought, *How can I already love you this much?*

These feelings of love and pleasure are the very same ones that your heavenly Father has for you every second of every day. His tender sentiments for you never change. You are that tiny, helpless baby in the outstretched hands of your heavenly Papa *all the time*. The stunning truth is that you can't do a single thing to make Him love you. He already does.

God loves you, not for what you do or don't do for Him, but because you are His. Period. He is positively thrilled with you!

He gazes upon you in total amazement and says, "My precious child, you have no idea what you do to Me. You are Mine. You're beautiful and you're everything I always wanted. When I made you, you were My dream fulfilled!"

Here is the truth of Papa's heart found in the Bible:

You must see what great love the Father has lavished on us by letting us be called God's children—which is what we are! (1 John 3:1 NJB)

[God] gives us the power to live, to move, and to be who we are. "We are His children," just as some of your poets have said. (Acts 17:28 CEV)

This is exceptionally good news! You are not *like* a child of God. This is not just a nice analogy to make you feel better. You *are* God's child. You are His actual son or daughter, created by Him in His image. Papa God has chosen you to be His very own, and with that come all of the rights of being in His family.

Paul explained God's outrageous love and affection for us this way:

How blessed is God! And what a blessing he is! He's the Father of our Master, Jesus Christ, and takes us to the high places of blessing in him. Long before he laid down earth's foundations, he had us in mind, had settled on us as the focus of his love, to be made whole and holy by his love. Long, long ago he decided to adopt us into his family through Jesus Christ. (What pleasure he took in planning this!) He wanted us to enter into the celebration of his lavish gift-giving by the hand of his beloved Son. (Ephesians 1:3–6 MSG)

Who is this extravagant Father? Who could possibly love you with that kind of passion? You were never an afterthought to God. You've always been on the heart and mind of your Father, who had plans for you to be here on the earth at this time and place in history before He even created the world. Just how important and special are you to God, whose creation of the world is secondary to His creation of you? He created you with the full intent to take you to "the high places of blessing" in Him and to saturate and soak you in His love and grace for all eternity.

His mind is made up about you. He has already settled on *you* as the focus of His love. He made this decision before you were born, before you had the choice to be loved in this way. So you'd better just get used to it—the sooner the better!

A Journey into the Center of God's Heart

Wholehearted agreement with your heavenly Father's massive love and full acceptance of you as His precious child will change your life dramatically in a way that nothing else can or will.

I grew up in a Christian home and was aware, in a general way, of God's love for me from the time I was a small child. In my early teen years, Jesus became real to me as a personal friend and I accepted the total forgiveness He offered me. At that point in time, I was born from above as a brand-new creation.[3] In my early twenties, I had a dramatic encounter with the Holy Spirit and He became as real to me as Jesus. In another book I'd love to describe my journey with the Holy Spirit in detail, because it's an integral part of my increased awareness of God's sweet presence. But for now let me say that in your own spiritual journey, it will benefit you immeasurably to become intimately acquainted with your heavenly Father, Jesus, and the Holy Spirit.

My journey eventually led me to become a pastor. I had several astounding encounters with God, and worshipping Him was a hugely important aspect of my life. Yet I often still felt like I was on the outside looking in, hoping I was doing enough and hoping He wasn't too disappointed in me because of my recurring failures.

The longing for a deeper connection with God, as well as a hunger for more understanding and experiences of the Spirit, launched me into a search that lasted for several years during the '90s. It took me to a variety of hot spots where God's presence showed up in a tangible way. I visited the Anaheim Vineyard, the Toronto Blessing, the Brownsville Revival, the Smithton Outpouring, the International House of Prayer in Kansas City, and many lesser-known places where the Holy Spirit was touching people in significant ways. The search was a good one in many ways, yet I still felt like I was always one experience shy of encountering God the way I truly wanted to. It seemed like everything I wanted was just outside my reach.

And then God in His goodness brought me through the most difficult period of my life, where all my hopes and dreams were shredded and became a tattered mess strewn behind me. (I'll explain more about this in chapter 5, "A Father Who Is Committed to Your Success.") I felt like a shell of a person, and I was fairly certain that I was a big disappointment to God. I was heartbroken. For months I found myself wandering in a spiritual daze, asking God the most basic questions: "You still love me, right? I'm still Your son even if I've messed everything up, right? You're not going to give up on me, right?"

In this extremely broken place, my Father began to show me the full extent of His unbroken promise to love me just the way I was. On one particularly memorable trip that I took to Canada, God met me while I was taking in the awesome wonder of Niagara Falls. It was a breathtaking sight to behold: colossal volumes of water sweeping past me every second, forcefully plummeting to the rocks below. My Father began to speak tenderly to my heart, *Son, My love for you is more massive, more expansive and more impressive than what you are looking at.* Tears welled in my eyes. He continued wooing me. *I have swept you into the current of My strong love, and nothing will take you away from Me. I will love you the way you deserve to be loved, and I will show you My affections in a way that's tangible and undeniable.*

I spent the following days in what I can only describe as a whirlwind romance, where God orchestrated my path to discover one beautiful Canadian park after another. We strolled together through these landscapes, just Papa and me, and He conveyed one simple message to the very core of my being:

I love you, Son!

But Father, I protested, *I've made quite a mess of things.*

His love was unrelenting. *Son, I love you when you are feeling like a success and I love you when you feel like a failure. I love you when you think you are being productive and I love you when you think life is passing you by. I love you just as much on what you perceive to be a bad day as I do on what you perceive to be a good day. I can't love you any more than I already do and I refuse to love you any less. I love you because I love you. I love you because you are Mine. I love you, and that's just the way it is and the way it's always going to be. I love you, Son!*

The Holy Spirit brought to life Scripture passages that I had read hundreds of times before, but suddenly were my Father's personal expressions of delight just for me.

> *Brent, I have loved you with an everlasting love and so I still maintain my faithful love for you.* (See Jeremiah 31:3 NJB)
>
> *Though the mountains be shaken and the hills be removed, yet my unfailing love for you, Brent, will not be shaken nor my covenant of peace be removed," says the Lord, who has compassion on you.* (See Isaiah 54:10 NIV)
>
> *But God, being rich in faithful love, through the great love with which he loved us, even when we were dead in our sins, brought us to life with Christ—it is through grace that you have been saved, Brent.* (See Ephesians 2:4–5 NJB)

I began to take in the heights and plumb the depths of my Father's love that Paul describes in Ephesians 3:14–19 (TMT):

> Overwhelmed by what grace communicates, I bow my knees in awe before the Father. Every family in heaven and on earth originate in Him; He remains the authentic and original identity of every nation. I desire for you to realise what the Father has given you from His own limitless resources, so that you may be dynamically reinforced in your inner being by the Spirit of God. This will impact your faith with capacity to fully grasp the reality of the indwelling Christ. You are rooted and founded in Love. Love is your invisible inner source just like the root system of a tree and the foundation of a building. (The dimension of your inner person exceeds any other measure that could possibly define you.) This is your reservoir of super human strength which causes you as saints to collectively grasp

(come to terms with, make one's own) the limitless extent of His love in breadth, in length, in height (rank), and the extremities of its depths. I desire for you to become intimately acquainted with the love of Christ on the deepest possible level, far beyond the reach of a mere academic, intellectual grasp. Within the scope of this equation God finds the ultimate expression of Himself in you (so that you may be filled with all the fullness of God).

I wept more tears of heartfelt gratitude and relief in those few days than I can ever remember weeping. The pressure was finally off! A huge load had been lifted from my shoulders that I didn't even know I was carrying.

Even though I had made some messy mistakes along the way, my Father wasn't disappointed in me at all.

Instead, He was masterfully using every circumstance in my life to bring me to a place of experiencing and accepting the unconditional love I'd heard spoken of so many times before (and I'd even preached about frequently as a pastor)!

Apparently, my life and my dreams had to crash and burn in order for me to realize a truth that I had never fully understood before: that I am accepted and approved of, regardless of my accomplishments for God or even the lack thereof. For the first time in my life I was completely free of that sinking feeling that everything I was searching for was just outside my reach. My Father let me know in no uncertain terms, *Son, your search is over. Every bit of intimacy you have longed for is yours. I hold absolutely nothing back from you. Come and enjoy Me as much as I enjoy you.*

Now, that was true freedom!

The love I discovered is the very same love your heavenly Father has for you. God is love.[4] Love is not just something He expresses, but it's who He is in His very essence. He cannot be other than who He is. Everything He does is motivated by love and saturated in love.

Take some time to share with God what is happening in your heart right now. Be as real as you possibly can—trust me, He can take it! Let Him know what you need to experience from Him in order to be whole and happy. Ask Him to show you who He truly is—not the God you thought He was, but a loving Father unlike any other.

Chapter Reflections

- What does it mean for you personally to know you are the Father's treasure? What difference does that make in your relationship
  with Him?

- How did it feel for you to say, "Daddy, You Love Me!"? If it was positive, ask Him to take you deeper still. If it was negative, ask Him to heal the places in your heart that make it difficult to receive His love.

- In your opinion, what is the most tender word for Father? Why? What fond memories are attached to that word? Try using that word right now as you talk with Him. Be real!

- Where has your search for God in your spiritual journey taken you so far? What still seems outside of your reach? Ask Papa to show you around in His kingdom where all things are yours.

- Ask the Lord to make Himself more real to you than He's ever been before.

Chapter 2

A Father Unlike
Any Other

❦

I am a good Father and I will always be
good to you every day of your life.
I am unlike any earthly parent you have
ever known—nothing whatsoever
like an abusive or neglectful parent
and far better than the best dad or mom you have ever seen.
The more you know Me, the more you will love Me and trust
Me.
But even as you are learning to trust,
My love for you never changes!

If I were to ask you to explain the immensity of the Grand Canyon to a three-year-old girl, it would be an impossible task, because a three-year-old child does not yet have the ability to make spatial jumps in her mind that are abstract in thought. You could say, "It's huge!" But to this little girl, so is an elephant. You could say, "Your whole town could fit inside of it," which would mean absolutely nothing to this child who has no clue about the size of her town, nor does she have the ability to equate that to a place she has never seen. The best thing you could do is to take her to the Grand Canyon and show her. While holding her hand, standing at the edge of this monstrous and awesome site, she would likely say, "Wow!" which might be the best possible description. Having seen it for herself, she now knows that the Grand Canyon is really, really big. But she still would have no description for it, either, other than "Wow!"

Similarly, how do we begin to comprehend and experience Father God, who is completely beyond our mental ability to fathom? When we say that God's love is infinite and unconditional, what does that mean? We are like that little child trying to take in something much too awesome to grasp. When we don't understand a concept, our brains try to locate something similar as a way of giving context to it. This is how we get some of the wrong concepts of who our heavenly Father is. The closest thing we think of is usually an earthly parent, grandparent, or possibly a pastor, teacher, or coach who played a significant role in our lives. While that's not bad if the person was especially loving and kind to us, it still falls woefully short of any true picture of how good God really is. And when those earthly models have done great damage to us, our concept of God as our Father often becomes extremely distorted.

The best thing I can do is to hold your hand and take you directly to the Father I have come to know well and allow you to see Him for yourself. That is the purpose of this book. It may very well be that once you get a glimpse of the real Father, you will only be able to say, "Wow!" But that might be the best possible description for Him. Even though your mind will never be able to wrap itself around all of who He is (otherwise, He would be smaller than you—not a good thing!) and you will never have an intellectual grid for fully comprehending the extent of His goodness, you will still be able to say, from the depth of your being, "Wow!"

Your spirit, however, has a direct connection with the Spirit of God at all times.[1]

This is why you can feel God's love even though it's beyond the ability of your mind to make sense of it all.

> You can experientially know truths to the core of your being about the Father's affection for you because of this Spirit-to-spirit direct line.

This is where that "Wow!" emanates from.

> His Spirit resonates within our spirit to confirm the fact that we originate in God. (Romans 8:16 TMT)

There Are No Limits to the Goodness of God

In the garden of Eden, when Adam and Eve enjoyed deep closeness with God, the serpent came and challenged them to doubt His goodness. That tactic has never changed. The same question must be answered in the midst of the uncertainties of life to this day. "Is God really good?" Your answer will determine your view of life and will affect the degree of peace and joy you carry in your heart.

The enemy doesn't want you to know the truth that you are never separated from God's heart of love.[2] Since Jesus already disarmed the devil by stripping him of his sham authority,[3] the only card the enemy has left to play is the deception card. If you believe one of his deceiving lies, he gains power over you with it. Your champion, Jesus, came to shine the light of His glorious truth into you, incapacitating the enemy's lies. Jesus continuously reveals the truth of the Father's heart by reminding you of who you really are as a son or daughter of the King.

By hearing and agreeing with the genuine voice of your Father who adores you, the old tapes of inadequacy will lose their power to hurt you. And you will be certain of the right answer to these questions that may have plagued you in your past:

Is God fed up with me or enamored with me?

Is He just putting up with me, or is He truly proud of me?

Is He looking to put me in my place, or is He a Father who's pleased with me and looking to build me up?

Does He enjoy watching me squirm and punishing my failures, or is He fulfilling His promise to victoriously lead me through this life into His awaiting arms?

Is God mad at me, or mad about me?

Personally, I've made my mind up about the goodness of God, with the overwhelming support of the Holy Spirit. This issue of God's unfailing, massive goodness is completely settled in my heart. That doesn't mean that I have all the answers to why certain things happen. Instead, I have a knowing in the depth of my being that God's goodness is far better than I can imagine and far bigger than I can see with my limited perspective.

If you are thinking that God is a little bit better and kinder than the best person you know, you are a billion miles short of the actual truth. Our Father is altogether other than anybody we know. He is perfectly good, perfectly kind, perfectly loving, and always for us, with infinite power to back it up.

One practical application of agreeing with God's goodness is choosing to disagree with your own assessment of yourself and your circumstances whenever it doesn't match up with the truth of God's goodness.

It's important that in your pain you don't build a case against the extreme goodness of God. It's equally important that you not tear yourself down, because you would be criticizing the one whom God adores and has perfectly crafted just the way He wanted. It doesn't glorify God one ounce to put yourself down or to feel bad about yourself. When you do this, you are agreeing with the accusing lies of the enemy. Once you get this truth of God's goodness for yourself, you will see others with His eyes, and like God, you will go on a faultless-finding mission!

One day all will be made crystal clear. And when it is, the goodness of God will never, ever be in question again. Until then, trust His promises:

> My joy will lie in them and in doing them good.
> (Jeremiah 32:41 NJB)
>
> Now to Him who is able to do exceedingly abundantly above all that we ask or think, according to the power that works in us ... (Ephesians 3:20 NKJV)
>
> I am the Lord, I do not change. (Malachi 3:6 NKJV)

What Lenses Are You Looking Through?

Whether or not you trust God and allow yourself to get close to Him has a lot to do with whether you want to. If you have a belief system that He is unsafe, manipulative, or prone to going off in fits of rage, you will avoid that relationship at all costs. That's called survival, and we were made with a degree of common sense not to put ourselves in perilous situations if we have a choice in the matter. However, since God is your Daddy who loves you, who is always for you, and who chooses to use His infinite power for your good, avoiding Him would be to your complete detriment.

We each view life through certain lenses that are colored by our experiences along the way. You read numerous truths in the first chapter of this book about the love your Father in heaven has for you, but how readily you believe those truths depends on what lenses you're looking through. If you had parents or other significant people in your life who misused their power to hurt you, it will be much more difficult for you to embrace the truth that God uses His unlimited power for your absolute best, to do you good all the time. If you were told growing up that you were good-for-nothing junk, believing the Father's comforting words that He's made you exactly the way He wanted and He likes you will be more difficult to accept. If you got the message growing up that whatever you did was never enough, your heavenly Father's voice of approval and acceptance will not initially seem to ring true.

The list of possible lies that some of you have been told, or abuses some of you have endured, would be too long and painful to address here, but can I tell you something you must hear? Every time a lie was spoken that tarnished your beautiful image, and every time your innocence was robbed because of an abuse of power, your heavenly Daddy wept for you. It is never His intent for the precious ones He loves to be damaged and taken advantage of. We have an enemy—the devil and his army of demons—who seek to destroy us. When we attribute everything that happens, good and bad, to God, we fall prey to the enemy's plan to steal from us the intimacy with God we were made to enjoy.

God is good and the devil is bad. It's critically important that we don't mix up these two facts.

God gives free will, which sometimes leads to pain and tragedy, but He also has a way of miraculously turning everything to our good as we stay engaged with our Father's heart through the process of restoration.[4]

Your Father knows every single thing that has happened in your life and He is more than able to override your pain with His love and compassion. He says to you, *I'm going to love you the way you deserve to be loved. I will treat you as the prince/princess you are until you believe it and hold your head up high as My priceless treasure.*

God is in the process of erasing the virus of past deceptions and lies from the hard drive of your mind and uploading you with His affirming words until you are left with your original programming. This will allow your operating system to function the way heaven designed it—clearly seeing the love of a Father who has always adored you and who has nothing but good in store for you. The amazing thing is, the more you receive His upgrades and believe them, the more you will live in the reality of His heart. I am declaring the truth over you right now that Papa God is giving you His lenses of love through which you can more accurately look at yourself and the world around you. You are receiving your upgrade at this very moment!

A Safe Papa

Recently, I was speaking about the Father's love at a conference. After my talk, Allen, a young man in his early twenties, approached me. He said, "When you explained how you would do anything for your sons and how our Father in heaven would do anything for us as His children, I had a really difficult time processing that. I found it hard to believe that there are fathers out there who would do anything for their kids. I had a dad who was abusive and who never showed affection. Whatever I did was never enough to please him."

Allen looked at me with an emotionless stare as he continued. "I have no grid for a heavenly Father who would do anything for me, because I never had an earthly dad who was that way. What can I do to experience God as a caring father like that?"

My heart broke for this young man because his story is all too familiar. He represents hundreds of people I have interacted with through the years who had a dad or mom who was alcoholic, violent, abusive, overly critical, impossible to please, smothering, controlling, or absent altogether. Far too many people have grown up in families that were chaotic war zones, where the best thing for a child to do was to duck and take cover. It would be difficult to adequately deal with these sadly all-too-common scenarios in this book, but these are the heartaches that the enemy seeks to take advantage of to keep us feeling trapped, lonely, and separated from the love of our heavenly Daddy.[5]

However, you have a Father who won't sit idly by and allow that deception to go on without breaking into your world to rescue you with His persistent affirmation.

Instead of hearing the old lie, *You'll never amount to anything,* you will hear your proud Father saying to you, *You're amazing and the sky is the limit for you, My precious child!* Instead of hearing the old tape in your head, *You're not doing it right, stupid,* you will hear the rejuvenating voice of your Papa, who says, *You're perfect for Me and you are doing so much better than you think. Keep going!* Papa will never shame you into behaving. Instead, He is the One who believes in you when you don't believe in yourself. He wants you to know:

> Even if you were abandoned, I will never leave you or forsake you.
>
> Even if you were not shown affection, I will lavish my love on you.
>
> Even if your father or mother was angry and yelled at you,
> I will speak tenderly to you.
>
> Even if your parents didn't seem to care enough to give you good boundaries, I will train you as My child to share in My own holiness.
>
> Even if you were rejected, I accept you as my own![6]

I looked compassionately into Allen's hurting eyes and shared truth with him. As it penetrated his heart, tears welled up. What I shared with this young man I also share with you. Your Father in heaven says to you:

> My dear, dear child. I love you with all My heart! My love is not manipulative, and I am not a harsh, impossible-to-please father. I was pleased with you before you could ever do a single thing to try to earn My affection. Come in closer and let Me demonstrate my unchanging love for you. Let Me wipe away the tears of the past that have kept you in bondage. It was never My heart for you to be mistreated by those to whom I gave responsibility to care for and protect you. I will love you the way you truly deserve to be loved. I will show you the perfect love and protection of a Father who always has your best in mind. I will take what the enemy meant for evil in your past and I will turn it into a life that is beautiful and meaningful. This will happen as I convince you of My goodness and as

you choose to receive My tender affection for you. I am the safe Daddy you've always wanted and needed. I have always been with you and I have always been for you. My heart will never, ever change.

Choosing to Forgive Imperfect Parents

God alone is able to turn what the enemy meant for evil into something very good in your life. He starts by giving you the courage to forgive your parents or others from your past who have wounded you so you can move into the fullness of His love. If you've been deeply scarred, you may feel a strong urge to skip over this section, believing the lie that you'll never be able to forgive the ones who have damaged your life. It also might feel terrifying to think about the possibility of stirring up painful emotions. For the sake of your freedom, please read on.

> Forgiveness is quite possibly the most powerful weapon the Lord has provided to break the chains of bondage the enemy wants to keep you shackled in.

Conversely, holding on to unforgiveness has been described as drinking poison and waiting for the other person to die. Unforgiveness constantly eats away at you (even when you think it doesn't) and robs your life of the peace and joy that God intends for you to have.

Let me explain what forgiveness is. Forgiveness is choosing to release another person from the hurt and offense that you've been carrying because of the injustice done to you. It is finally releasing that person from the debt of owing you anything for any injustices that have happened to you. There's a freedom in doing this that you can't imagine until you take the plunge and actually do so.

Now let me explain what forgiveness is not. Forgiveness isn't agreeing that what happened was okay or acceptable behavior. Forgiveness is also not giving an unsafe person permission to continue hurting you.

One of the primary reasons for choosing not to forgive someone is the sense that justice will not be served. But by not releasing that person, the pain of the injustice becomes a constant companion and the wound never truly heals. The unfortunate consequence is that pain leads to more pain. The very pain that you are holding on to eventually hurts others you love, even though that's the last thing in the world you'd want to do.

Yet all it takes for life and blessing to be passed along, instead of pain and heartache, is for one person to break the chain. The cycle of pain can stop with you if you choose to forgive the past injustices done to you and accept the love of your heavenly Father, who fills all the empty, hurting places. By refusing to empower the pain, abuse, and lies of your past, and by wholeheartedly embracing Papa's great big heart for you, others whom you love will experience His blessing right along with you.

By choosing to let go of the right to demand your own justice, you'll be able to experience something that's much greater—finally enjoying the life of love and peace that you're made for. If we're honest, we don't really want justice if that means paying for all we've done wrong too. None of us wants what we deserve for our own mistakes— we want the mercy and grace of Jesus! And that's exactly what Jesus wants for you. On the cross, while dying in our place for sins He never committed, Jesus compassionately cried out, "Father, forgive them for they know not what they do."[7] Instead of giving us what we deserve, our Savior gladly gives us what He purchased for us on the cross: forgiveness, mercy, and love. Jesus then implores us, "What you've freely received, freely give!"[8]

Forgiving someone who has severely hurt or abused you is not just difficult—it's impossible. However, Jesus came to make impossibilities possible.[9] You can't imagine how proud Papa is of you for being willing to forgive the wrongs of another. How He longs for you to let go of this weight that has been far too heavy for you to carry.

He says to you:

Just as I hold absolutely nothing against you, and because I have made you in My image, you can, by My strength, choose to hold absolutely nothing against another. Heaven is cheering you on because of the victory you will experience in releasing the ones who hurt you.

You don't need to speak directly to the ones who hurt you. (In many cases there would be denial of any wrongdoing, and in some cases the person is no longer alive.) But I do encourage you to speak to them as though they were present. If this is particularly difficult, ask the Holy Spirit to help you. When you are ready, you can say something like this out loud:

> _____ (Name), I forgive you for all the pain you caused me in my life. (Be specific about what you are forgiving this person for. It really helps to get it out.) I forgive you for not being able to love me and protect me the way I needed and the way I was supposed to be loved and protected. I forgive all the injustices you committed against me. I forgive you for not being able to see the treasures in me. I release you from your debt of owing me anything in return. I hold nothing against you. I choose to bless you and not curse you. I release you completely to Jesus. You are free to go. My heavenly Father will meet every need that I have.

I encourage you to speak this out loud, releasing as many people as you need to forgive. Then take a deep breath and celebrate what's just happened, because ultimately, you've just released yourself! I've seen countless people experience life-changing transformation by forgiving others in this way. By choosing to forgive, you've just taken away the enemy's greatest weapon to hold you down. You are free to experience more and more of the love of your Father you were designed to enjoy.

If you were not yet able to forgive, I encourage you to take the next step by being really honest with the Lord and telling Him about it. He knows anyway and He doesn't love you any less. Ask for His help to do what you cannot do. You might want to pray, "Lord, I'm willing for you to make me willing to forgive."

If your wounds came primarily from your mom or a mother figure in your life, you might be wondering, *How can God as a Father fill in those gaps I have for a nurturing mother?* Let me assure you, God is fully able to meet those needs as well. The Bible says that male and female were both created in His image. This means that when we look at both the masculine and feminine qualities of human beings, we have a much fuller understanding of who God is. One of the names of God is El Shaddai, which means "The All-Sufficient One" or "The Many-Breasted One" (the Hebrew word *Shad* means "breast"). God is able to nurture all of his children adequately. The Lord says:

> Can a mother forget the baby at her breast and have no compassion on the child she has borne? Though she may forget, I will not forget you! (Isaiah 49:15 NIV)

Picture yourself as a baby being perfectly nurtured by your mother, receiving all the nutrients you need from her milk (which even contains antibodies to protect your body from disease). You feel safe, warm, wanted, and comforted. This is a true picture of El Shaddai, who sees you as that vulnerable child wrapped up in the secure yet gentle arms of Love, and who gently says to you:

> I know you can't take care of yourself without Me. I have great compassion for you and I will take tender, loving care of you, providing for you all of your most basic needs for security, affection, and the comfort of a mother's touch. Shhhh ... be still in My arms and let Me sing My lullaby of love over you.

To you who are overcoming past hurts, I speak a blessing to your spirit and cleansing to your wounds, asking the Lord to graciously heal the depths of your pain permanently in Jesus' name.

Grace Is for Parents Too

Not one parent in all of history, apart from our heavenly Daddy, has been a perfect parent to his or her children. If you are a parent and feel remorse for how you've treated your own children, I have some really good news. God's grace is for you too! Your Father has forgiven you. In addition, it's vitally important for you to forgive yourself. God holds nothing against you, but you might be holding yourself captive by refusing to forgive yourself for not being perfect. God has never expected that from you. This would be a good time to say out loud, "I forgive myself for not being perfect." Then you can watch the chains fall away from you. Go ahead!

> When you make mistakes, let your children know you made a mistake and ask for their forgiveness.

Then affirm them over and over again. Let them know how loveable they truly are. Even if your children are grown and have left your house, it's not too late to apologize to them. Ask for their forgiveness and speak words of affirmation to them. If, in their pain, they're not able to forgive you just yet, let God work on their hearts for a season. Your willingness to be real about your own imperfections will be a huge deal and will be part of their healing path. Choose to love and encourage them from this point onward. The more you take in the Father's love, the more pure love and affection you will have to pour out to your children. That's the way it works!

Papa says to you:

> If you feel you've made a mess of your life and your relationships, you need to know that I specialize in turning things around and restoring what you may think is beyond repair. I am so much bigger than your mistakes! I am the One who turns the hearts of the parents to their children and the hearts of the children to their parents.[10]

Finding Earthly Spiritual Fathers and Mothers

Although I grew up very loved and affirmed by my parents, I had a need for earthly spiritual fathers as well. At one point in my ministry, I experienced a time when I felt like a complete failure. In that season of life, I discovered a man named Bill Johnson, who carried the same spiritual DNA I had but who was much further down the road, providing a path for me to follow. The first time I heard Bill communicate his heart and passion at Bethel Church in Redding, California, I knew that my search for a spiritual father had ended. Kris Vallotton, also from Bethel Church, became another spiritual father for me and a source of life and inspiration, continually speaking words of encouragement and destiny into my life. I felt my dreams resurfacing. I had permission to soar again. I am beyond grateful for these two men whom the Lord placed in my life to affirm me and from whom I have inherited multiplied blessings and favor.

I believe that all of us need earthly dads and moms who are deeply connected to the Lord, who can give us the "two thumbs up" of affirmation, and who give us permission to be who we were truly created to be. Our own earthly parents may fill this role, or God may bring other spiritual parents into our lives, or both. I strongly encourage you to ask God to bring men and women into your life who truly have your best at heart and who want to see you launched into your destiny as a world changer.

If you heard words of negativity or abuse growing up, listen to your Father in heaven, who is speaking the only words you need to hear and receive:

> My child, you are everything I've ever wanted! When I made you, you were My love dream fulfilled. You measure up. You are enough. My voice is the only one that matters. I will speak words of tenderness and affirmation to you. My love and acceptance will completely transform you. I am the safe, adoring Daddy you've needed your whole life, and I'm here to shower you with My affection. Come in closer and hear My voice of approval.

Chapter Reflections

- Does knowing that your spirit and God's Spirit are connected at all times change how you view your relationship with Him? Why or
why not?

- Where has it been a challenge in your life to believe God is really good?

- Where have you seen God change a difficult circumstance into something surprisingly good in your life?

- Where specifically do you need to disagree with your own assessment of yourself and your circumstances that don't align with the truth of God's goodness?

- How would you describe the lenses you are currently looking through in life? What lenses do you want to be looking through? Ask Papa for the ability to do so.

- Does God feel safe to you? If not, what words would you use to describe how you feel about Him?

- Were you able to forgive a parent or another authority figure who didn't treat you as the true treasure you are? What emotions and feelings did that elicit?

- If you are a parent, what did the Lord reveal to you about restoring your relationship with your child or children?

- Do you have earthly spiritual dads and moms? Who are they? Have you talked with them about it so that they're aware of the place they have in your life?

Chapter 3

A Father Who Likes You and Wants You

My child, I have called you by name and
I have purposely chosen you to be Mine!
I have always wanted you to be with Me,
and I want to be with you forever.
I like you! I like you a lot.
I like everything I made about you—the color of your eyes, your
infectious laugh, the quirks that are uniquely yours—everything!
I like hanging out with you, whether we're doing
something or doing nothing together.
I enjoy looking at you—you make Me smile.
Let's enjoy life a whole lot more together.

As you read these words from your Father, you may feel a clash within you, especially if you have not heard these kinds of words before. Yet they are true. Yes, your Father loves you, and He also *likes* you. Not because He is forced to, but because you are altogether loveable and likeable! The clash within, if it exists, comes from an errant, distorted view of yourself that you picked up along the way. Let's face it—we are all our own worst enemy and critic. To the degree we've bought into the lies that we are defective and without value, our own thoughts about ourselves unjustly condemn us, and we inadvertently continue the cycle of reinforcing those lies. We need to press the heavenly Refresh key and receive both a new, updated picture of our Father and a clarified view of ourselves as Daddy's chosen ones.

Do it Again, Daddy!

I've loved playing with my boys at every age of their young lives, but some of my most tender memories are of my interactive play with them in their early toddler years, when I would show them my love and affection mainly through my touch and eye contact. We could play a simple game over and over again without it ever getting old, like when I would lie flat on my back and hold them straight up above me with outstretched arms, face-to-face, so that our twinkling eyes locked onto each other. After an anticipatory moment of waiting in that position, I would quickly collapse my arms and engulf them into my chest. They would squeal with delight and I would giggle right along with them in utter joy! They would say to me, "Do it again, Daddy!" I needed no coaxing. I would immediately hoist them up for another round of affectionate play. Just thinking about it all these years later instantly brings me back to the sweetness of those adorable toddlers of mine, making me laugh all over again.

My boys didn't have to twist my arm to make me do that. They didn't beg me and bug me until I somehow relented against my will. No. The truth is, I wanted to have fun with them, because I absolutely loved being with them and laughing with them. They couldn't keep me away even if they tried (which, of course, they didn't). At first, I had to initiate the playful love because they hadn't experienced it before, so how could they know? Once I gave them the experience of how much fun I could be, there were times when they would approach me and initiate the playful encounters. Either way, it was every bit as fun for me as it was for them.

How much more your heavenly Father enjoys you! His tender affection for you isn't something He has to conjure up, and He certainly isn't waiting for you to beg Him to give you some attention. This is the way Papa's heart always is toward you. He had to initiate true love first or you wouldn't even know what it was. But the more you experience His genuine affection, the more you learn to initiate fun times with him. Either way, your Papa adores you.

> Wild horses couldn't drag Him away from you! He wants to be with you—not just for this moment—but for every moment throughout all eternity.

Forever Is a Very Long Time

Your heavenly Father will never, ever grow tired of you. Why would He grow weary of the very one He created just the way He wanted?

Our Father created each of us with the full intent that we would be with Him forever in His heavenly kingdom. What father, full of perfect love, would create children with the express purpose of being separated from them for all of eternity? That makes no sense whatsoever. Yet this is how our heavenly Father is often portrayed. In fact, the Father's will is clearly stated: He wants no one to be lost and everyone to be brought to repentance.[1]

Though some perceive that our names are written in the Book of Life when we trust in Jesus as our Savior, I would offer a different view. Our names were already written in the Book of Life from before the foundation of the earth. This is one of the renderings of Revelation 13:8. This understanding is also consistent with Jesus' saying that He will never blot out the names of His conquering ones from the Book of Life.[2] He didn't say He would add us after we have conquered.

This distinction makes all the difference in the world. If our names have already been written in the Book of Life, that clearly portrays a

Father who has always wanted us and who would never have created us with the intent of being separated from the very ones He loves.

Am I saying that all roads lead to eternal salvation? Absolutely not. Jesus is the way, the truth, and the life.[3] His is the only sacrifice that makes us perfectly right with the Father. Do we still have to choose God and accept Jesus' sacrificial gift of paying for our sins on the cross? I believe we do, and I will explain my response in chapter 8, in the context of a loving Father who covenanted Himself with us long before we could respond.

You've always been God's choice. If that doesn't blow your circuits, I don't know what will.

> God chose us in Christ to be holy and blameless in God's presence before the creation of the world. (Ephesians 1:4 CEB).

You were never an afterthought to God. He did not create the earth and then think, *Hmmm ... I guess I should put people on this planet to complete the project.* No, you were on His mind and in His heart before He created this earth.

He didn't create you for the purpose of simply populating the earth. He created the earth for you to rule over and enjoy with Him.

If my own sons were in danger, I would do everything in my power to protect them. God does have all power, and He willingly uses it on our behalf. Since He has determined in His heart to have us with Him forever as His very own, He left nothing to chance. That's why He sent Jesus to purchase us for Himself. He says, "I must have *you,* because you are of infinite worth to Me!"

> For you know that it was not with perishable things such as silver or gold that you were redeemed from the empty way of life handed down to you from your forefathers, but with the

precious blood of Christ, a lamb without blemish or defect.
(1 Peter 1:18–19 NIV)

As my dear friend Art Fuller loves to remind me, "You are more valuable to God than Himself!" If you stop and think about that for a minute, it will make your jaw drop in wonder and awe. *I'm more valuable to God than Himself?* Yet that's an accurate assessment of your true worth. It's God's assessment, and He is always right!

Once you allow yourself to agree with such outrageous assertions of the Father's love, your heart will soften. And then it will get all stirred up with the excitement of making up for lost time when you thought for all these years that He was angry, distant, or disinterested in you.

By the way, don't get upset with yourself, with others, or with God if this revelation is just now starting to sink in. Papa has a way of giving you back above and beyond anything you feel you have been cheated of in the past. All He really wants is your heart from this point onward. Once you give Him that, you are well on your way to a life of happiness you never dreamed possible.

Your Father's gaze is always upon you because He wants to be with you, longs to be with you, even needs to be with you. Some would have a problem with this, saying that God has no needs, that He is completely sufficient unto Himself. While I would agree that God is not deficient in any way, still, love chooses to need another. That's why love is risky. God chose to put His love on the line for us by acting first and declaring His outright love and desire for us. He boldly did this without a single guarantee that we would want Him in return. But that's what true love does!

Adoption

You are always on your Father's heart and mind, and He didn't make the choice lightly when He determined to take you as His own. In Ephesians 1:5 an interesting word is used to describe the method of how he chose you.

God destined us to be his adopted children through Jesus Christ because of his love. This was according to his goodwill and plan. (CEB)

That word *adoption* has very special significance. Some have the impression that adoption is akin to being a second-hand choice, but in the culture of the day when Paul wrote this, adoption wasn't taken lightly at all. The adopted child was given all the rights and the inheritance of the firstborn.

When we were adopted as God's very own, we were instantly given all of the rights of the Firstborn of all Creation, who is Jesus![4]

In the book of Hebrews, we are described as a church of firstborn sons who are surrounded by countless multitudes of angels.[5] By knowing we are adopted as the Father's choice, that wayward orphan spirit we once carried is permanently changed to a spirit of adoption.

> What you received was not the spirit of slavery to bring you back into fear; you received the spirit of adoption, enabling us to cry out, "Abba Father!" The Spirit Himself joins with our spirit to bear witness that we are children of God. And if we are children, then we are heirs, heirs of God and joint-heirs with Christ. (Romans 8:15–17 NJB)

Though we are called adopted "sons," this is a non-gender-specific term that Paul used to describe all of God's sons and daughters, just as "the bride of Christ" is used in the Bible to describe not just women, but all men and women who are betrothed to Jesus as our forever Husband and King. While the terminology may seem odd at first, heavenly realities are much deeper than the shadows of meaning that we have on the earth.

A Love that Never Gives Up on You

Knowing your Father wants you as His very own forever and He likes who you are, it becomes obvious He can't and won't ever give up His pursuit of your heart. That means you can make the worst choices imaginable and still not be disqualified from His attentive care and love for you. Sometimes people who have been badly wounded in life learn to sabotage relationships as a protective measure. In a way, they are saying, *Since we're getting close and I don't want to be hurt, I will hurt you first and drive you away so I don't have to experience the pain of your rejecting me.* Such wounded people do the same in their relationship with God. What they don't count on is the persistent, even stubborn nature of God's love that outlasts them. Our amazing Daddy refuses to take no for an answer.

In the parable of the lost coin,[6] Jesus describes a widow who relentlessly searches her house for this misplaced coin until she has found it, and then she throws a big party. Jesus makes it clear this illustrates the Father's heart for His children. Every child who forgets who he or she is and wanders away from his or her inheritance is searched for until found—not a casual search, mind you, but a continual, relentless one. Make no mistake, the Father knows right where His wandering children are. But this story was told to convey the extravagant measures God will take to pursue you.

> Your beauty and love chase after me every day of my life. (Psalm 23:6 MSG)

Every one of us has tried to run from God's love in one form or another. Often it's because we don't feel deserving of His love, so we figure we'll just spare Him the trouble of having to cut us off by cutting ourselves off first. The problem with this strategy is that God will never cut you off, nor will He allow you to cut yourself off. The other fundamental flaw of running from God is that wherever we run away to, He's already there!

> Where shall I go to escape your spirit? Where shall I flee from your presence? If I scale the heavens you are

there, if I lie flat in Sheol, there You are. If I speed away on the wings of the dawn, if I dwell beyond the ocean, even there your hand will be guiding me, your right hand holding me fast. I will say, "Let the darkness cover me, and the night wrap itself around me," even darkness to you is not dark, and night is as clear as the day. (Psalm 139:7–12 NJB)

Just because we run from God doesn't change His heart toward us—not one little bit.

If it did, we would all be in deep trouble. His love will wear you out! If you are like a kicking, screaming child having a temper tantrum of sorts, He will hold you until you get it all out and finally fall limp and exhausted into His strong arms that never let you go. Even depression or suicidal thoughts and actions cannot keep Him at a distance. Do you think when you are at your worst and when you need Him the very most He would choose that time to pull away from you? It won't happen, because Papa God is 100 percent committed to you and to loving you through every moment of your life. Whether you feel Him or not, the reality of His presence and His devotion to attending to you never changes.

No Fear of Punishment

You cannot trust someone who intends to hurt you. Because of misconceptions about God's heart, some who truly want closeness aren't able to open themselves up to Him out of fear, especially the fear of punishment. That fear paralyzes them from any ability to experience intimacy.

I've been surprised to discover how many believers live gripped with the fear of being punished one day for all their mistakes. On the one hand, they believe they're forgiven because of Christ's sacrifice for them on the cross, yet there's also an underlying fear that they've messed up too badly and punishment awaits them. How can both be true? They can't!

God is love. It's true that God loves, but the deeper truth is that He *is* love. God can do nothing outside of his character—outside of who He is. And who He is, to the core of His being, is love. Everything He does is consistent with His nature. Therefore, God only operates in love and everything He does is motivated by His great love.

Why is love so important to disarming the fear of punishment? Take a look at 1 John 4:16–19 (NJB):

> We have recognized for ourselves, and put our faith in, the love God has for us. God is love, and whoever remains in love remains in God and God in him. Love comes to its perfection in us when we can face the Day of Judgment fearlessly, because even in this world we have become as he is. In love there is no room for fear, but perfect love drives out fear, because fear implies punishment and no one who is afraid has come to perfection in love. Let us love, then, because he first loved us.

John, who wrote this, walked with Jesus while He was alive on the earth and experienced the genuine love and grace that flowed from Him. John also encountered the resurrected Jesus, whose eyes of blazing fire consumed him with love.[7] This is why there is such urgency in John's letter for us to relate to Jesus and the Father He came to represent in love, and not with an inferior motive of fear. In effect, John is saying, "Having had many encounters with this man of pure love, if you're still afraid to meet Jesus or relate to His Father of love, believing you don't measure up, you haven't gotten the immensity of God's love yet, and you haven't understood why Jesus went to the cross for you."

Love is the one motive that brings lasting change! We can be motivated by many other things in an attempt to relate rightly to the Lord (fear, guilt, shame, pride, etc.), but these are all extremely short-lived. Living from the motivation of the fear of letting our heavenly

Father down is not His plan for us. Being made in the image of God, who is love, the only motivation that will feel genuine for us is love.

Love requires a choice. Our Father's love for us was His choice and He desires for us to choose to love Him in return.

If we were forced by God to love Him because He's bigger and stronger and will punish us if we don't, that's not love at all—that's manipulation. True love does not manipulate. So God chose to level the playing field through His Son, Jesus, on the cross. With the poison of sin's curse on humanity neutralized by the perfect sacrifice of Jesus, we never again have to approach God with the fear of punishment as our frame of reference.

> [Jesus], on the other hand, has offered one single sacrifice for sins, and then taken His seat for ever, at the right hand of God, where he is now waiting till His enemies are made His footstool. By virtue of that one single offering, he has achieved the eternal perfection of all who are sanctified. The Holy Spirit attests this to us, for after saying: No, this is the covenant I will make with them, when those days have come. The Lord says: In their minds I will plant my Laws, writing them on their hearts, and I shall never more call their sins to mind, or their offences. (Hebrews 10:12–17 NJB)

And earlier in that same book:

> There will be no further need for each to teach his neighbor, and each his brother, saying "Learn to know the Lord!" No, they will all know me, from the least to the greatest, since I shall forgive their guilt and never more call their sins to mind. (Hebrews 8:11–12 NJB)

We're now living in the days that were spoken about in these passages, because Jesus has already come and created the massively transformational shift to the new covenant of grace by His death and resurrection. (I'll expound on this in chapter 8.) Since God has declared He will remember sin no more, we can now approach Him face-to-face and choose to be in relationship with Him based solely on love.

What About Sin?

You may be thinking, *But isn't sin still a problem? You aren't telling me God doesn't care about that, are you?* Honestly, He cares so much about having a kingdom of righteousness that He left absolutely nothing to chance. He took the sin problem head-on by dismantling its power over us through the work of Jesus on the cross! And if that weren't enough, He put His *Holy* Spirit right inside of us, doing for us what we didn't have the power to do without Him. Yes, God cares! He cares deeply. Our Father loves us tenderly, which is why He hates to see sin destroying His children or the fabric of the loving community He's designed for us to enjoy. He's always pleased with who we are, but He's not always pleased with the hurtful decisions we make when we forget who we are and walk in a way that is inconsistent with our brand-new nature in Christ.

At this point, many will revert to a legalistic, perfectionistic mindset. *Since God's not happy with everything I'm doing, I will live mistake-free so He's never mad at me.* How quickly we can go there, but to what end? How has it worked for you, trying to get yourself straightened out for God? He's not impressed with your attempts to do that, because He knows you can't.

You can't make yourself right with God. You are right with God because of Jesus' perfect payment on your behalf on the cross.[8] God isn't mad at you, nor will He ever be.

Ask yourself this question: *Was the payment of Jesus' blood on the Cross enough?* If the answer is no, none of us can be saved. But if the answer for you is yes, then begin living in the freedom and joy of His free gift of salvation!

It is absolutely clear that God has called you to a free life. Just make sure that you don't use this freedom as an excuse to do whatever you want to do and destroy your freedom. Rather, use your freedom to serve one another in love; that's how freedom grows. (Galatians 5:13 MSG)

God, your Father, did not create you to punish you. He created you to love you. Just in case you skipped right over that, I want to tell you again. You were created, not so that God could find ways to crush you for your disobedience, but so that He could find as many ways as possible to lavish His deep affection upon you.

For God so loved the world that he sent his one and only Son, that whoever believes in him shall not perish but have everlasting life. For God did not send his Son into the world to condemn the world, but to save the world through him. (John 3:16–17 NIV)

When we hear about Father's affection and adoration for us, a part of us reels back in disbelief because we are instantly aware of all the reasons He shouldn't love us. Each of us is extremely aware of our own shortcomings and we easily fall into the trap of feeling unworthy. This is where Jesus comes in. Without a Savior, yes, we would shrink back with feelings of shame. But that has been gloriously taken care of with Jesus' sacrificial death on the cross. In a word, Jesus has made you *unpunishable*.

It's time to melt in Daddy's arms and once again agree with His heart for you:

My child, you are My absolute joy! You are everything I ever wanted. I miss your company when you wander, but I am never angry with you. My Son, Jesus, took all of that away forever for you.

It's time that we go places together that I've planned for a very long time. It's time to set your sights in the direction of My kingdom alone. You are great beyond measure and I've been building you up to believe this. I'm making you believe this because of where we are going together. I've given you great favor and I've massively blessed your life. I've loved you with an everlasting love and I will maintain My love for you forever. There is no end!

You and I are on a journey—climbing mountains, forging streams, flying above the clouds, even hiking deep ravines and valleys. It's a great adventure and I will never leave your side. You are My beloved child and I love you. Always have—always will!

Get to know Me even more. I'm far better than anything you've experienced thus far and even what you've spoken to others about Me. But find out why. Go deeper still. This is a brand-new phase of your journey with Me. Trust Me. Enjoy Me! I have such plans for you: plans to touch the world through you … plans to release the oppressed … plans to draw you in deeper and to have you sit longer in My refreshing, restoring presence as I share My secrets with you about Myself and My kingdom.

I love to share My secrets with the ones I love. That includes you, My precious child!

Chapter Reflections

- How does it feel to be liked by God? List at least ten things you think He likes about you. The list has no end, by the way, so list as many as you can!

- Picture yourself as a child enjoying Papa God as He enjoys you in a setting that is fun and safe for you (a picnic, an amusement park, on a swing, blowing bubbles, etc.) He really is a fun Dad. Allow yourself to linger there with Him as long and as often as you want to!

- What does the phrase "I'm more valuable to God than Himself!" do to you?

- If you take fear of punishment out of the equation in your relationship with Papa, how would you like to approach God? What does an unpunishable relationship look like? What will it give you the courage to do in life?

Chapter 4

A Father Who Celebrates You

❧

My child, you are absolutely amazing.
I don't tolerate you—I celebrate you!
I call over the angels in heaven to point you out and brag on you.
And why shouldn't I?
I made you in My glorious image and I did a fantastic job.
You are My treasure! You are My delight!
I look at you and I am amazed at what I created.

Papa gives us this picture into His heart for us:

> Yahweh your God is there with you, the warrior-Saviour. He will rejoice over you with happy song, he will renew you by his love, he will dance with shouts of joy for you, as on a day of festival. (Zephaniah 3:17 NJB)

The prophet Zephaniah was looking ahead to a future day when Israel could enjoy this exuberantly happy God in this delightful way. The "day of festival" here refers to when the Messiah would come to bring their long-awaited salvation. The Messiah has come, and we are living in that day of the Father's exuberant happiness over us now.

We don't have to wait any longer to enjoy our boisterous Daddy, who unashamedly calls out to all who will listen, "I'm a proud Papa. Just look at my astounding kids!" If you listen even more closely, you will be able to hear from heaven, "Waaaaaa-hooooooo!" You've probably guessed what that is … it's His excitement over you reverberating throughout the cosmos. Knowing that God is cheering you on with His wild, celebratory love will renew you like nothing else can.

God Can't Contain His Excitement

Several years ago, I got a clear picture of how God dances over us as His highly cherished kids. While I was walking through the streets of Jerusalem with some friends, we witnessed a wedding party marching through the streets. Let me tell you, they were having a wildly great time and they hadn't a care in the world about who was watching. They were lost in the sheer exhilaration of the moment. The sound of the clarinets and tambourines rose up as the wedding party and guests shouted, danced, and clapped their hearts out. The joy was so contagious that some of the bystanders jumped in and joined in the extravaganza.

This is the same culture in the midst of which Zephaniah was writing. When this passage says that our Father dances over us with shouts of joy, it's talking about an unrestrained, all-out celebratory bash that goes on and on. *This* is your Father, who is tremendously excited about you! If you didn't know this, meet your true Father. And listen again to His shout over you:

> W a a a a a a a a a a a a a a a a a a a a a a a a a a - hooooooooooooooooooooooooo!

A Doting Father

When my oldest son, Derek, was a few months old, he made the cutest cooing sounds as he was waking up in the morning. My wife, Suzanne, and I would hear him and then get out of bed and quietly tiptoe over to gaze through the crack in the door and watch with utter delight as our son looked around and made the most adorable gurgling noises. I can't tell you how precious he was! After a time, we would push the door open, enter the room, and sing over him an exuberant, silly "good morning" song. You'll have to use your imagination to hear us sing:

> Good morning! Good morning!
>
> Good morning, Jesus loves you!
>
> Good morning and we love you too, too,
>
> Boop-boop-de-doo!

The moment we started singing, his eyes began searching the room for us until he spotted us. Then he squealed with delight when our eyes met. Needless to say, our hearts melted on the spot and we swooped him up in our arms with total joy. Of course, we did the same with our second son, Aaron, fully enjoying those precious moments with him as well.

Your Father in heaven gazes on you all the time. Not so He can spy on you, but because He can't take His eyes off of you.

Yes, God is smitten with you!

I can picture Him calling the angels over to Himself, pointing toward you, and saying:

> Hey! Come take a look at my awesome son. He's remarkable. He's stunning.
>
> Would you just look at my amazing daughter? Wow! She's beautiful. Just looking at her takes my breath away.

And then He begins to sing His love song over you.

> He will rejoice over you with happy song. (Zephaniah 3:17 NJB)

As His song fills the air with tender words of adoration and approval, you search for the origin of that sweet voice. Then you squeal with delight:

"Oh, Papa! There you are. You *love* me!"

When you gaze His way, you completely melt His heart, and He savors the moment. One glance from you makes His heart go pitter-patter. Really!

> You ravish my heart, my sister, my promised bride, you ravish my heart with a single one of your glances. (Song of Songs 4:9 NJB)

You're Beautiful and Then Some

The poetic book of Song of Songs provides vivid imagery of passionate love between the king and his beloved that is an accurate portrayal of the Lord's love for us. In Song of Songs 6:4–5 (NJB), He says:

> You are fair as Tirzah, my beloved, enchanting as Jerusalem.

That may not seem all that romantic until you learn that Tirzah means "agreeable" and "pleasant," and that Jerusalem is called "Perfection of Beauty" and "the joy of the whole world" in Lamentations 2:15 (NJB). Therefore, the One who loves you dearly is saying to you:

> You're perfect for Me, My beloved. You are pleasing, and you bring Me endless joy and delight. The beauty of who you are is intoxicating to Me.

If you are turning around, wondering who He's talking about, I want to challenge you to look in the mirror and ask God to give you His eyes to see yourself the way He does. Then look even more intently to see the beautiful princess or handsome prince standing before you, and hold your head up higher, knowing that you are royalty and you are deeply cherished.

If you do not yet see yourself as the immensely valuable treasure you are to God, I have another truth to add to the arsenal of flabbergasting love bombs sent your way to convince you. When the author of Hebrews writes about Jesus, "For the joy set before him he endured the cross, scorning its shame,"[1] the joy he's talking about is *you!*

What?

Yes, you were the joy set before Jesus that gave Him the courage to endure the cross. He saw Himself and His Father in the future, along with all those He so dearly loved that He rescued them from darkness, together forever.

If the joy set before Him was only being back with the Father, He didn't need to leave heaven in the first place. He was already with the Father before coming to the earth. No, His prize was clearly you!

Revelation like this absorbed into your spirit will change you from the inside out. Why don't you tell Him right now how it makes you feel to know that you were the joy set before Jesus on the cross?

Papa Delights in You

One morning I woke up with the line of a song playing over and over again in my head that reminded me of God's delight to pour His goodness down upon us. I began to ponder why He would so willingly choose to do this. Why, even when we are unfaithful, does our Father persist in faithfully showering us with His goodness and mercy? The question lingered in my mind throughout the day, so I finally asked out loud, "Father, why do You so faithfully set Your affection on me like You do?"

I heard in response, "Because of the delight it brings to Me!"

You see, our Father is a pleasure seeker, and we are the ones who give Him that pleasure. I may have woken up that morning thinking about the goodness of my Father, but He already thinking about me the entire time I was sleeping. And He never stops thinking about you, either. In the Psalms, David said the thoughts of God, which are more numerous than the grains of sand on the beach, are precious to Him.[2] Can you imagine the immensity of our God, who is love, to have continuously flowing thoughts of love and affection and desire for each of His children throughout all eternity? It boggles the mind, which is why we will never enter into the fullness of His love by trying to wrap our finite minds around it.

I urge you to plunge into the depths of Daddy's love without putting a safety harness on. Explore the vastness of His affections toward you and don't worry if you never find your way out again. Soar into the expanse of the limitless kindness and goodness of the One who loves you with an everlasting love, and give yourself permission to never come down out of the clouds! God made us for one major purpose: to enjoy Him. That's what He wants us to do more than anything else.

True lovers need someone to love. God is the truest of all lovers, and that someone would be *you*!

You are the one who gives God pleasure. You make Him smile. You have captured His heart. You are the one He must have as His own forever. You are the most loved person in the universe because your Daddy says so! Return His affections and warm His heart with yours today any way you can!

He will start by saying:

> My child, you are amazing! Inspiring! A delight! A joy to look at and be with. You cause My heart to dance, to sing, to leap with gladness because you are exquisitely made. I formed you with pleasure and fashioned you with pride. You are My finest creation—one that I choose to intertwine Myself with for all eternity. Yes, you! You make My heart beat faster each time you glance at Me. You turn Me inside out when you choose to worship and love Me.

You are the one I love and adore and cherish and treasure ... it's *you*!

Now it's your turn to return the love and affection!

Jesus Is our Model

If you are still finding it difficult to accept the Father's love, let's take a look at how He loves His Son, Jesus. About Jesus, the Father says:

> You are my son, today I celebrate your birth! I am to you all that a Father can be to a son, and you are to me all that a son can be to a Father. (Hebrews 1:5 TMT)

At Jesus' baptism in the Jordan River, the Father couldn't contain His excitement and burst out:

> This is My Son, whom I love; with him I am well pleased. (Matthew 3:17 NIV)

Wow! The Father's love and pleasure for His Son was announced publicly. Jesus' identity was completely wrapped up with the certainty of His Father's approval, which is why He was so easily able to openly declare to all, "The Father loves Me!"[3] He wasn't trying to impress anyone with that statement, and He certainly didn't need to convince His Father. He knew what He knew to the core of His being, and was totally secure in it. "My Daddy loves Me!"

Jesus' life on this earth was a perfect demonstration of gushing out the love He was taking in from His Father.

Before His death, Jesus prayed a stunning prayer to His Father:

> I have made your name known to them and will continue to make it known, so that the love with which you loved me may be in them, and so that I may be in them. (John 17:26 NJB)

Did you catch that?

> The love the Father lavishes on His Son, Jesus, is the very same love the Father has for us. *The very same.*

I don't know any Christian believer who would have a problem believing the Father loves His Son, Jesus. Therefore, it appears we are completely out of excuses as to why or how God couldn't love us.

Have you ever heard of a prayer Jesus prayed that didn't get answered? His prayer that we would receive the very same love He received from His Father and that He Himself would be in us has been answered already by God, with an emphatic "Yes!"

> His grace-plan is to be celebrated: He greatly endeared us and highly favored us in Christ; His love for His Son is His love for us. (Ephesians 1:6 TMT)

Your Father Cares

People who genuinely love you sincerely care about you. Your heavenly Father is extremely interested in your life and cares about you more than you could imagine. Your Father cares about what you are doing, as His Word reveals:

> [Lord], you examine me and know me, you know when I sit, when I rise, you understand my thoughts from afar. You watch when I walk or lie down, you know every detail of my conduct. (Psalm 139:1–3 NJB)

He cares about where you are going, even when you aren't aware of His presence:

> However faint my spirit; you are watching over my path. (Psalm 142:3 NJB)

He cares about the little things.

> Can you not buy five sparrows for two pennies? And yet not one is forgotten in God's sight. Why, every hair on

your head has been counted. There is no need to be afraid: you are worth more than many sparrows. (Luke 12:6–7 NJB)

He cares about the big things.

They woke [Jesus] and said to him, "Master, do You not care? We are lost!" And he woke up and rebuked the wind and said to the sea, "Quiet now! Be calm!" And the wind dropped, and there followed a great calm. (Mark 4:39 NJB)

Your Father in heaven cares about *you*!

Do not be afraid, for I have redeemed you; I have called you by your name, you are mine. Should you pass through the waters, I shall be with you; or through rivers, they will not swallow you up. Should you walk through fire, you will not suffer, and the flame will not burn you. For I am Yahweh, your God, the Holy One of Israel, your Saviour. ... I regard you as precious, since you are honoured and I love you. (Isaiah 43:1–4 NJB)

This is why He says:

I am telling you not to worry about your life and what you are to eat, nor about your body and how you are to clothe it. ... Can any of you, however much you worry, add a single cubit to your span of life? If a very small thing is beyond your powers, why worry about the rest? ... Set your hearts on his kingdom, and these other things will be given you as well. There is no need to be afraid, little flock, for it has pleased your Father to give you the kingdom. (Luke 12:22–32 NJB)

He not only cares about you and about everything you are going through, but by His covenant love, He has chosen to use His unlimited power on your behalf every moment of your life. That's what the favor of God looks like.

You're Daddy's Favorite—Get Used to It!

Everybody wants that special feeling of being someone's favorite. Perhaps you had hopes as a child of receiving a special Valentine's Day card from that one you especially liked sitting across the room in grade school. But whether or not you've ever felt singled out as someone's favorite in your life to this point, you are most certainly Daddy's favorite. And He has a very special valentine picked out just for you. For you men, you are Dad's "sport," His "champ," His prince. For you women, you are Daddy's girl, His sweet princess ... and you always will be.

You may be thinking, *God has a lot of children. How can He have more than one favorite?* I would reply, *You're missing the point.* God has plenty of love to make every child His favorite, but the only way you get to experience all the benefits of being His favorite is if you actually believe it.

One of the benefits of being Daddy's favorite is that there is always more for you!

There are layers of the Father's love, just like being toasty warm under layers of down comforters on a cold night.

John 1:16 says, "From his fullness we have, all of us, received—one gift replacing another" (NJB). The Emphasized New Testament says that we have received "favor after favor." Barclay's New Testament says there has come "wave upon wave of grace." The Twentieth Century New Testament says we have received "gift after gift of His love." These all convey the unending treasure of the Father's extravagant love for us, free of any effort on our part. Since God certainly isn't going to take away yesterday's blessings, today's mega-dose of His love must certainly be added on top of His previous blessings!

If you have received "cold" words from somebody lately, simply pull on another layer of Daddy's oozing love for you, like a warm blanket. If circumstances have left you a bit dismayed, go back to the place of peace by basking in another layer of comfort that comes from Daddy's heart to yours. If you have been driven by yourself or someone else to be perfect, accept Papa's assessment that "You are enough and you measure up!"

The more you are aware of the extreme favor you carry as a child of the King, the more you will soar above the clouds with the joy of being His, no matter what the circumstances. I encourage you to say out loud:

"I'm Daddy's favorite, and that's just the way it is!"

By the way, here's His Valentine's Day card for you:

My Beloved,
You are Mine and I am yours *forever*.
You are so very precious to Me.
I can't stop thinking about you.
You are perfect for Me, exactly what I wanted!
I want My love for you to make you totally secure—
nothing will ever come between us.
Because of that, My love for you will never, ever end.
I have wonderful surprises waiting for you.
I sing songs over you all the time to fill you up with joy.
I am fascinated with you,
and I am singing over you at this very moment.
I approve of you and I really enjoy being with you
every moment of every day,
including this very moment.
And this one.
And this one…
Come away with Me, My beloved, My lovely one![4]

~ Papa God

Daddy's Kisses

I remember a trip our family went on to an amusement park and on the way home we stopped for pizza. My almost-two-year-old niece, Isabella, was with us and she had crashed with exhaustion after a long, fun day. She was completely zonked out, snoozing on her mom, Kiyana, who was lovingly looking at her precious daughter and saying, "I love these times because I can kiss Isabella as much as I want to." Of course, she was referring to the fact that a nearly-two-year-old has a bundle of squirmy energy that doesn't lend itself to slowing down long enough to receive too many kisses. And now Mom had her chance!

As soon as she said this, I thought, *What a perfect picture of how our Daddy in heaven loves us.* We are precious to our Father and He thoroughly enjoys watching us run around and discover things. But since we are often too active to enjoy His kisses, He can hardly wait until we get to the end of our day, exhausted and needing rest. Then Papa says, "Oh, good! Now I get to kiss them as much as I want to." You see, God never sleeps nor slumbers.[5]

What do you suppose He's doing when we're sleeping? Well, since God is love, it makes perfect sense that He takes that time to kiss us as much as He wants to. And just like Isabella, you don't have to do a thing to receive those kisses. It's simply the natural response of Daddy's perfect love that must find its expression toward the ones He adores—that's you and me!

No wonder we wake up with a fresh gift of new mercy every morning.[6] It's because we had huge doses of love lavishly and continuously poured out upon us all night long. Jeremiah 31:3 (BBE) reads:

> My love for you is an eternal love: so with mercy I have made you come with me.

God has a definite motive for showering us with His love. Here it is: Since God knows He's the best thing for us, He makes it downright impossible for us to resist Him, and we find ourselves continuously drawn into His great heart.

If you think this is good news, I have some even better news for you. You don't have to wait until nighttime for your heavenly Daddy to kiss you. God is always showering us with His love and He is bringing us into a growing awareness of His love during our waking, active hours as well. In fact, one of Paul's most fervent prayers is that we will truly get how big and good God's love really is.[7]

This is why it's so important that we slow down and enjoy "soaking times," when we learn to tune our hearts to His and experience more and more of that continuous flow of love. Why don't you take a few moments right now to quiet your heart and agree again with the most powerful truth the world has ever known: "Daddy, you *love* me!"

> He does not merely tolerate you politely, He delights Himself in you! (Ephesians 5:29 TMT)

Chapter Reflections

- What does it do to you to know that you bring extreme joy to the heart of your heavenly Father?

- Quiet your mind for a moment and listen to the song that God sings over you. Hear the laughter in His voice as the melody bathes you in His love and delight.

- If your main goal with God is to enjoy Him, what might your times with Him be like?

- Agree with God that you are extremely lovable. Now ask Him to explain why that's true about you.

- What excuses do you need to deposit into the trash about why God couldn't or wouldn't love you?

- Knowing that God cares about even the smallest of things that's important to you, is there anything you want to talk with Him about right now that you used to think would bother Him if you brought it up?

- Go ahead and say out loud, "I'm Daddy's favorite!" What benefits do you get to enjoy from that being true?

- When and where have you experienced Daddy's kisses from heaven lately? Ask Him for a kiss today and for the awareness not to miss it.

Chapter 5

A Father Who
Is Committed
to Your Success

&

My child, you measure up. You are enough.
My Son, Jesus, made sure of that for you.
I did not make you deficient in any way.
I approve of you!
I have plans for your life to be wildly successful,
but let Me define success—
and enjoy the journey with Me!

When I was about five years old, I fell asleep in the back of our family station wagon on one of our long trips to our cabin in the Santa Cruz Mountains. With a family of six, my dad and mom sat up front, my oldest sister and brother were in the middle seats, and my other sister and I (the two youngest) were able to lie down flat in the cargo area in the back (long before current seat-belt laws!). I distinctly remember two things.

My first remembrance is of the deep hum of the car as I lay my head down on the pillow that lulled me to sleep. The second is the complete absence of any worry, because my Dad was driving. I didn't need to know where we were in the journey, if there was enough gas in the car, or any other concerns. I knew my dad would take all of us to the place we were so looking forward to going. I didn't have a care in the world as I was nodding off, because I knew that when I awoke, I'd be safely at the cabin to experience lots of fun times together as a family.

Enjoying the Journey

God, our Father in heaven, is a genuine family man. He loves to take His children places, and He has fun doing it. And one thing I have come to believe with all my heart is that He knows how to get us there safely! Ultimately, we're going to be with Him forever in the most fun place imaginable.

In this life, when we're tempted to fear the journey, all God's asking us to do is lay our heads down, listen to the deep hum of His heart beating, and know with child-like trust that He will take us safely to the next destination.

Yes, there will be bumps in the road and difficulties at times, but we have an amazing Daddy who loves us more dearly than the most loving earthly father who ever existed.

He is the One who says to us:

"I will let them sleep secure." (Hosea 2:20 NJB)

He is the One who is driving us to one destination point after another until we reach our final destination with Him forever.

Your God continued to support you, as a man supports his son, all along the road you followed until you arrived here ... going ahead of you on the journey to find you a camping ground, by night in the fire to light your path, and in the cloud by day. (Deuteronomy 1:31, 33 NJB)

And He is the One who knows how to get us there safely.

To him who can keep you from falling and bring you safe to his glorious presence, innocent and joyful ... (Jude 24 NJB)

There Is No Plan B

Two of the greatest needs we have as humans are the need to be loved and the need for significance—for our lives to make some kind of real difference in this world. God created us with both of those needs built right into us, and He has every intention of fulfilling them perfectly. Interestingly, the two are intricately connected. Knowing and experiencing His full and unconditional love is essential to fulfilling our purpose of accurately representing Him to the people He places in our path along life's journey.

> When I look at where God has brought me to in my life, I can truly say that He is masterful at orchestrating events, even seemingly negative ones, into a brilliant plan, getting me to exactly where He wanted for His divine purposes.

I am convinced that God does not have a plan B in mind when we seemingly make a major mess of His plan A. He is way bigger than that! He uses every single event to patiently instruct us and shape us into the likeness of Jesus, to love the way He loves, and to usher in His heavenly kingdom of power on the earth. Not every day of our lives looks like that plan when we attempt to analyze how we think we're doing. But our Father, who created time for our sakes but lives completely outside of the constraints of our chronological timeline, says to us:

> Step back a moment, My child, and see the bigger picture from My perfect perspective. I am at the beginning and I am at the end, and I am at every point in between at the same time. Every moment in time is "now" for Me. Before a single day of your life came to pass, I knew each and every moment that would take place for you. I see you as you already are. I see the finished product, and I like what I see! I know how to get you where I want you to be because I am already there with you. You will have to trust that what I have started in you I will most certainly complete in you.[1] Yes, you have free will that causes certain outcomes, but I have already taken those outcomes into account. I have no plan B for your life, only my singular plan A to do in and through you everything I have promised I will do. I am revealing My true nature to you bit by bit, and you are being changed from glory to glory as a result.[2]

Our Father, our Daddy in heaven, has an absolutely perfect plan for the life of each and every child of His. He takes painstaking care to address every detail of our lives to His complete satisfaction.

> He pre-designed and engineered us from the start to be jointly fashioned in the same mould and image of His son according to the exact blueprint of His thought. We see the original and intended shape of our lives preserved in His Son; He is the firstborn from the same womb that reveals our genesis. He confirms that we are the invention of God. Consistent with His definition of our lives, and our original spirit identity, He declared us righteous and restored His glory in us. (Romans 8:29–30 TMT)

Notice how all of the emphasis is on what God will do in your life and how He will get you there. This is nothing short of astounding!

Perfectly Orchestrating My Life

Growing up, I really wanted to be a small-animal veterinarian. Keeping my eye on that goal, I worked diligently in veterinary offices throughout high school. I became the president of our local 4-H club, even spending one summer raising a sheep that I sold in an auction at our county fair. I went to college at the University of California at Davis to get my undergraduate degree in zoology. Although I had given my life to Jesus much earlier in life, I rediscovered Him in college—or should I say, He recaptured my heart in a way that was irresistible.

My grades in college weren't good enough to be accepted into the extremely competitive veterinary graduate school at UC Davis. Although I was disappointed, I chose to continue my pursuit of the love of animals. While finishing my undergraduate degree, I worked with various species of monkeys at the UC Davis Primate Center. Then I landed an animal lover's dream job at Marine World Africa USA in Redwood City, California. I performed in the educational Ecology Theater show and helped to raise three tiger cubs from infancy through four months (by which time they had already reached a weight of sixty pounds!). I also got to handle llamas, arctic foxes, caracals, ferrets, boa constrictors, opossums, and numerous other critters. Truly this was an animal lover's paradise, yet I didn't feel quite settled that this was what I was alive for.

During that same time, I was helping in the junior high ministry at my church and saw the impact I was having on these young people who were searching for answers and desperately needing affirmation during their awkward preteen years. I felt a deep satisfaction walking alongside them, helping them to make sense of their journey with God. It became increasingly apparent to me that I received much more fulfillment from helping and encouraging people than I did from training animals.

Let me say at this point that each one of us has particular gifts and passions and desires to make a difference in this world. We were made that way. My point here is not to say that working with people is more significant than working with animals, but that I was discovering who I was fashioned to be.

God used my desire of being a veterinarian to lead me down a path that eventually led to a new dream of ministering to people. I am keenly aware that none of my years working with animals was wasted. I enjoyed that part of my journey immensely. I often counsel people to take steps to go after their dreams, because even though they may not see them fulfilled the way they imagined, God has a way of perfectly orchestrating life events to redirect them right where He wants.

My life was showered with favor at every turn as I continued on the path that my Father laid out before me. He consistently encouraged me at just the right time so I wouldn't give up.

Following my new passion of becoming a pastor to lead people closer to God, I pursued a three-year Master of Divinity degree at Fuller Theological Seminary in Pasadena. During the first year, I married my college sweetheart and best friend, Suzanne. Aside from choosing to follow Jesus, this was the best decision of my life! In His extreme goodness, God gave me the perfect woman to enjoy life with.

Before the completion of my seminary degree, I began interviewing for various church pastor positions. In two churches, I was one of their final candidates but was not the one chosen for the position. I was now just two months away from graduating. My anxiety level was increasing. I candidly reminded God, *You know that I'm married and that I have to take care of my wife, right? And You know that I only have two months until I graduate, right? What am I going to do?* In that state of worry (let's call it what it was), I went to sleep one night and had a dream that changed the course of my life.

In my dream, Jesus walked right up to me, dressed in a white robe. He looked directly into my eyes and asked me, *Brent, do you love Me?*

I immediately responded, *You know that I do, Lord!*

He replied, *Don't worry. I have a place for you.* As He said that, He reached out and touched me. The exact moment His fingers made contact with my body, I lit up with an electric white light that consumed me from head to toe. It was His glorious presence, jolting my body like a million volts of a heavenly current! At that moment I woke up from the dream, instantly wide awake and still completely lit up with that heavenly white light. All I could do was lie there and weep because of the immensity of the glory of the Lord's presence resting on me.

What happened next was nothing less than a miracle. Just days after graduating, I was hired by a church in Pleasanton, California. The church hadn't even heard of me prior to the dream I had, but in less than two months, they chose me as their associate pastor in a process that often took a year or more to complete. I am certain to this day that Jesus cleared a path in front of me and said, "There you go! This is where I want you."

During the time I was at this church, I continually pursued Jesus with all my heart and I began experiencing the miraculous side of God in a way I had never known before. Since that time, I've seen hundreds of amazing miracles as blind eyes, deaf ears, paralyzed spines, and numerous diseases were completely healed in the powerful name of Jesus! A few of these stories I will share in subsequent chapters.

God also used this time to open my eyes to truly appreciate the diversity of the entire body (family) of Christ, not just those whose beliefs were identical to mine. He deposited in my heart a huge desire to see unity in the family of God the way He sees it. As a result, I've developed deep friendships with many other pastors in my region.

After seven years, some unfortunate events in our church led to the entire staff being asked to resign. Though I wasn't personally involved in the events, I was certainly impacted by them. I can look back now and see how God was nudging me out of the comfortable nest I had built for myself there.

At this point I thought I was going to leave the area and find a church in another region to lead. Apparently, my heavenly Father had other plans.

Suzanne and I were at the movie theater in 1997, watching the remake of *The Preacher's Wife*, when, in the midst of the show, the

Holy Spirit fell upon me in a dramatic way. Suddenly, it was just the Lord and me all alone together in the middle of a crowded theater. The movie faded away and the Lord had my complete attention. I received a ten- to fifteen-minute heart-to-heart straight from Papa's heart to mine.

He said to me, *Brent, My son, it's crucial that you not only believe in Me, but that you also believe what I say to you. I want you to stay in this region. I have plans for you here.* I had no idea what that meant or what it was going to look like, but because of my history with my undeniably faithful Father, my response was *Yes, Lord!* He also told me to read Hebrews chapter 11, because He had something He wanted to tell me.

Later, while poring over what the Lord had instructed me to read, I came to verse 8: "It was by faith that Abraham obeyed the call to set out for a country that was the inheritance given to him and his descendants." (NJB) God said to me, *Stop! I want you to claim your inheritance right here in this region. This is where I have supernaturally called you and this is where I want you to flourish.* So right then and there I put a spiritual stake in the ground and claimed my inheritance.

When God gives us clear promises about our future, He's providing for us a remembrance stone to embrace when our current circumstances don't appear to line up with where we think we should be. The message of God's relentless love I would be releasing to the world still had to be chiseled into the very core of my being through some extremely painful life lessons. God gave me the future promises ahead of time so I wouldn't give up.

After receiving this clear promise from God about staying in our region, Suzanne and I decided to take a big risk. We would start our own church. We were tremendously excited and scared to death at the same time. This was my first attempt in life to launch my own venture and I was determined to host the presence of God in a church where people would flourish. We had some amazingly fun and powerful times in that church, admittedly learning a lot by trial and error. However, due to some irreconcilable differences amongst the leadership team, I left that church after four years feeling like a failure and a big disappointment to God. Suzanne and I were deeply wounded in the process and we hurt others deeply as well. It was, relationally, the most painful season of our lives.

Yet, out of that time of crushing pain I learned invaluable lessons about myself and about the faithfulness of my Father. I learned that my identity can never come from what I do, but must only be rooted in the One to whom I belong. I learned that trying my hardest to be God's perfect son was no substitute for resting in the security of Papa's great heart for me. I learned that unless I immersed myself in the Father's love in a much deeper way, I would hurt people and cause pain even when I had no intention of doing so. I learned that my task as a pastor was not to build a church (which Jesus already did), but to expand God's kingdom through a family culture of love, grace and honor.

As I explained in chapter one, Papa brought a deep restoration to my heart during this devastating time through His unrelenting approval and affection. He continually affirmed me as His loved and wanted son until my dreams resurfaced. Suzanne and I would spend hours a day soaking in Daddy's love, sometimes crying with overwhelming gratitude in our hearts that He still had good plans for us. He gave us courage to continue the journey.

Learning from our past and looking forward to our future, we started Blazing Fire Church, living the dream God planted in our hearts to live. We are still pastors of that church today. As a church family, we are discovering that the more we enjoy the Lord's presence, the more it transforms us, spilling out effortlessly to a world of people who are desperately hungry for the love of a Father.

A few years after starting this church, I was walking on a hiking trail in the beautiful coastal mountains of California where God spoke to my heart something I will never forget. While pondering some of my crushed dreams in the previous church, I heard my heavenly Daddy say, "I want you to thank Me for everything that's happened in your life. If those things hadn't happened you wouldn't be the person you are right now."

Suddenly, all the pain the Lord had faithfully walked me through had a purpose. I could see how this experience changed me. I knew His love in a way I couldn't have known it before going through this difficult season in my life. Papa was inviting me to live a life completely free of bitterness, disappointment, and regret where I could clearly see His good and perfect plans unfolding over my entire life.

Here I stand, still in Pleasanton, two-plus decades after Jesus came to me in a dream. By encountering God's love in a deep way through the ups and downs of my journey, He's imparted to me a huge heart for loving and encouraging people. He's given me a strong desire to gather and encourage pastors and ministry leaders in my own region and throughout the greater San Francisco Bay Area.

The Lord spoke a very clear word to me a few years after arriving in this region. He said, *My Spirit will sweep through this valley and this Bay Area region with or without you. Do you want to be part of it?* My answer has continuously been a resounding "Yes, Lord!" It's most certainly happening, and the sweet presence of His Spirit is continually escalating.

Our Father means what He says: "I know the plans I have for you. Plans to prosper you and not to harm you. Plans to give you hope and a future."[3] This is the true heart of our Papa. This is His true heart for you.

He is not disinterested in your life, or simply a casual observer, but He is intricately fashioning the details of your life to produce a beautiful fragrance that attracts others to the source of that beauty.

He includes you in everything He's doing, not because He needs to, but because He wants to and chooses to. He is the proud owner of a Father-son/Father-daughter construction company with you!

Your ultimate destiny has an end point in being together with your Maker and Companion face-to-face, but your journey along the way is also part of your destiny. If your destiny is only an end point, then you miss the joy of all of the moments along the route your Father intended for you to travel. I'm still walking out my destiny and at every stage of my journey, my Daddy has been there to encourage me, steady me, redirect me, and even pick me up and get me going again when needed. Every one of us needs that direction from a caring Father. And He's more than happy to provide it. His covenant promise to us is "I will work everything—absolutely everything—for your good because I love you."[4]

God invites us to see the world and our own history from His perspective. He says, *Child, climb up onto My lap and see the whole picture as I see it with the sealed-up victory of your life in plain view!*

I encourage you to take some time with Papa right now, sitting on His lap and asking Him to review your history with you—including what you perceive to be your failures—from His perfect perspective. Be amazed at His outrageous faithfulness, not shamed from any poor decisions you have made. If your life doesn't seem to be in a good place right now, ask to see it with His eyes and ask Him for encouragement about what's just up ahead on your path.

> The path of the righteous is like the first gleam of dawn, shining ever brighter until the full light of day. (Proverbs 4:18 NIV)

Supplying All of Your Needs

When my son, Derek, wanted to learn to play the bass guitar with the hope and desire of playing in his Christian high school worship band, I was genuinely excited for him and wanted to help make it possible. I had him do some research on new and used bass guitars to find out about sound quality, reliability, extra features that he may want, and, of course, the prices of various guitars. I took him to a music store, where he tried out several of them until he found a certain five-string bass that suited him. His smile told me that he'd found the one he wanted. I was thrilled to go up to the register and purchase the guitar and accessories that Derek needed, knowing that it was going to help him go after an awesome dream of his.

He not only played in the school worship band his junior and senior years of high school, but on many occasions he joined our church's worship team as well. Because I played acoustic guitar on the team, I'd look over at times with extreme joy, watching Derek jam alongside me. Every once in a while, our eyes would meet with laughter in them. We were worshipping our King together and having a blast doing it!

Your heavenly Papa puts amazing dreams inside of you, and He has every intention of helping you fulfill your dreams.

It's His joy to do so. In fact, His dreams for you are so big, they are completely beyond you without His help. That's purposeful, because His plan is to be the supplier of absolutely everything you need.

> God has the power to cause all kinds of gifts to overflow to you, so that you will be wealthy in all things at all times, and will have much left over for every good work. God who fully supplies every single expense, plus more, to pay for the seed for the sower, and to pay for all the expenses for bread to the eater, will supply all the expenses to pay for, as well as multiply, the seed you sow, and make the crops of your righteousness grow. (2 Corinthians 9:8, 10 TSNT)

According to Dr. Ann Nyland, the verb for "fully supplies every single expense, plus more" (*epi-khoregeo*) refers to the paying of all expenses, every single one of them, even additional, unplanned expenses.[5] In other words, no stone is left unturned. The word is the same root word used for fifth-century Greek drama where a private citizen, known as a *khoregos,* would vie for the great honor of paying for the entire drama—elaborate stage sets, costumes, training, whatever was needed. The expenses were hefty, but it was considered a huge privilege to pay the costs to make it all happen. At the end of the drama, the *khoregos* would be brought forward to the thunderous applause of the crowd as a huge thank-you for making it happen.

Our Father is the One who knows every word of every scene of every act in the drama called "our lives." He considers it His great honor and huge privilege to pay for what is needed on your behalf. And not just what you need to get by, but to include the added touches—the extra kisses from heaven—to show you His good, generous, and benevolent heart.

A day is coming soon when we will all be with God and see how our lives were perfectly woven together in this story of Christ through the ages, in which we each were given a significant part to play. And we will rise as one in a thunderous ovation of gratefulness to the One who supplied everything we needed to do our part and to get us home safely.

Yeah ... He's *that* good!

When our Father promises that He will finish what He has started in us, His confidence is in Himself and the ability He has to take care of everything necessary to get us to where we are supposed to be.

Take a deep breath and enjoy the journey!

But What If I Fail?

Do you ever get to the point where you wonder why God puts up with you? Where you feel like a failure because you've fallen again? Take in this massively encouraging word:

> When a person's life pleases the Lord, He gives them a sure footing; they may fall, but they never fall down, for the Lord holds them by the hand. (Psalm 37:23–24 JMT)

You are that person who pleases the Lord. Jesus purchased you for your Father in heaven at the cost of His blood. You are in perfectly right standing with God and you please Him because you are His!

His promise of giving you sure footing doesn't mean you never stumble or trip up; it means He doesn't allow you to crash and burn. The New American Standard Bible (verse 24) says, "When he falls, he will not be hurled headlong, Because the Lord is the One who holds his hand."

God gave me an amazing vision while meditating on this verse. I saw a child who had tripped and I instantly saw the Father's strong hands lovingly grasping both hands of the child steadily above the child's head. The child had his eyes closed in fear and said, "Daddy, I can't get back up." Then the view panned back until I could see that the Father was holding the child in the air above the ground even though the child thought he was still on the ground. The Father said gently, "Child, put your feet down and touch the ground that's beneath you." The child opened his eyes and with great relief slowly lowered his feet to the ground while the Father continued to hold his hands.

> This is a picture of what it means to be a favored child of God—not that you have your act together and never stumble, but that your heavenly Daddy has you as secure as you could ever be.

God is not looking on to see if you get it right—He is actively involved in your journey, making sure that He gets you to the finish line victoriously! God doesn't just "put up with you," He delights in you. You are most certainly not a failure, so never align yourself with that lie. You are God's success story. The fact that it doesn't always look that way to you only goes to prove how amazing God's covenant of grace truly is. He wants you to know this:

> There are many more chapters ahead of you in your life that you haven't lived. I can't tell you all about them yet,

but they're really good ones. I know, because I'm already there to see it. Keep going! Never give up! Trust Me that I have the big picture in mind at all times. Not just the big picture for your life, but I also see how everyone's lives intersect with all of My purposes for history. It's all going to end up just the way I intended. You keep going on the path I've placed before you and keep asking Me for My counsel every step of the way.

Turning Failure into Victory

Peter was one of Jesus' closest friends, and he promised Jesus that he would never abandon Him, no matter what. When Peter failed miserably at standing up for Jesus in His darkest hour, he felt like a dismal loser. So much so that even after he had seen the living, resurrected Jesus, he went back to his previous trade of fishing because he didn't think Jesus would have use for him anymore. Peter's failure was fearing for his own life on the night of Jesus' brutal arrest, leading him to deny knowing Jesus three times when questioned by the Romans around a charcoal fire.[6]

Why do you suppose John would have mentioned in his gospel that it was a charcoal fire? The answer is clear when you read about the charcoal fire Jesus built after His resurrection to cook fish for the disciples who were out fishing all night.[7]

Jesus intentionally brought Peter back to the same atmosphere of that charcoal fire to give him the opportunity to come through with flying colors this time.

In order to restore Peter from defeat to victory, Jesus asked Peter to affirm his love for Him three times. Jesus didn't scold him. Jesus never even asked Peter why he denied Him. He simply said, feed my sheep and take care of my lambs.[8] Jesus was telling him, in effect:

Peter, I know you feel bad about what happened, but feeling bad isn't going to get you to where I need you to be. I know all things. I know that you love Me, but you needed to hear yourself say the words so that you would believe it again. I brought you back to the charcoal fire—to the place of your failure—for you to succeed this time. I have things for you to do, Peter. I have taken away any and all excuses for disqualification. You are Mine, and you know My love for you. It's time to get back in the game. I need you to feed people the truth of My grace and love. I need you to take care of those who have lost their way and point them back to the Father I revealed to you, Peter—a Father who wants each and every child with all of His heart.

The Lord then used Peter in astounding ways ... the very same man who at one time thought he was unusable. Just look at the next chapters of Peter's life and see the rest of the story.

In Acts 2, after the Holy Spirit comes in power, it's Peter who gets up and preaches to the crowd, and three thousand people come rushing into God's kingdom that day! In Acts 3, it's Peter and John who stretch out their hands and heal the crippled man at the gate called Beautiful, and it's Peter who once again speaks to the crowds and two thousand more people are drawn into God's kingdom. In Acts 4, Peter is no longer bound by fear or unbelief. He is put in prison for preaching the good news of Jesus, and even when threatened with his life, continues to tell the enraged council about Jesus. In Acts 5, the power and glory of God are pouring out of Peter—even his shadow is healing people! In Acts 9, it's Peter who heals a paralytic and, as a result, everyone in the towns of Lydda and Sharon want to follow Jesus. Also in Acts 9, it's Peter who raises a woman from the dead, and many in the town of Joffa choose to believe in Jesus. Peter ends up so free from his past fear and doubt that he is sleeping soundly between two guards while imprisoned in jail when an angelic jailbreak sets him free. Peter's past didn't disqualify him. God's love for Peter and His determination for Peter to walk out his destiny prevailed.

The same is true for you. You are loved and you are accepted.

No matter what you have done, no matter how much of a failure you feel you've been, you are never disqualified from God's kingdom. Jesus has prequalified you to share in His inheritance.

Keep going, and look into the eyes of the One who says to you, "You can do it! I am holding you up and giving you My strength for the journey."

Allow the Lord to love on you and burn away the things that have no business being in a new creation in Christ Jesus. Whether or not you end up preaching to crowds where thousands are saved, the Lord has chosen you and is perfectly preparing you to love as He loves and to make a huge difference in His kingdom.

Believing that you are a failure, a loser, or God's "project" is only agreeing with the accuser. You belong to only One, and the opinion of that One who affirms you is the only voice that matters, Someone who is continually down on him or herself is not readily available to be used by God to lift up others. But someone who knows his or her infinite worth will have one encounter after another in which the encouragement of God flows freely through him or her, making a huge difference in the lives of others. That's your destiny, beloved!

Listen once again to the voice of your Daddy in heaven and make a choice to agree with what He says about you:

> My child, I know everything about you and I've always known you've needed a Savior—that's why I sent My Son to die for you and that's why I've left nothing to chance. If you've forgotten who you are, I'll remind you and bring you back to the path of life where you were designed to walk.

You're not a failure; you're My success story! Wait until you see the next chapters I've written unfold in your life.

You're not a disappointment; you are a treasure to Me. I invite you to look in the mirror and see what I see. Every time I look at you, I say, "Wow!" because I am enamored with you. Actually, you so capture My heart that I can't take my eyes off you!

I tell you again: you're not a failure. Don't ever listen to that lie. When I made you, I knew exactly what I was doing and I am thrilled with what I made! I want you. Come, rest your head on My chest and hear My heart beat for you. Listen closer. It sounds like this:

I love you ... I love you ... I love you ... I love you ... I love you ... I love you ... I love you ... I love you ... I love you ... I love you ... I love you ... I love you ... I love you ...

... and it goes on like this for eternity!

God says He's made you an overcomer, but to experience that, you have to overcome something. So, no matter what impossible-looking obstacle seems to loom large in front of you, remember God is always positioning you to succeed. Preparing their children for success is what any good parent would do, and our heavenly Daddy is not just "any good parent." He's the ideal parent, who is perfect at loving and encouraging you into your amazing destiny.

Be encouraged that only good is going to come to you from your Father. This is why King David could sing:

When you win, we plan to raise the roof and lead the parade with our banners. May all your wishes come true! That clinches it—help's coming, an answer's on the way, everything's going to work out. (Psalm 20:5–6 MSG)

Unfolding Grace

Papa is your greatest supporter and encourager.

He intends for you to rise to the top, to soar into your appointed destiny, to finish strong in this race to receive your gold medal with Him on the winner's stand.

And He knows along the way it can be very hard. If you have been feeling overwhelmed, discouraged, or disillusioned in any way, I want to bring you encouragement straight from the throne of God.

First of all, I want to assure you that through the battles, your Father is strengthening your ability to believe and trust Him in ways that would boggle your mind. Run into the arms of your loving Father, who has always wanted you and who will never give up on you. Go to that place of intimacy with God, no matter what it takes. Ignore the discouragements and enjoy the huge heart of the One who adores you. Lay your frustrations and anxieties on the One who has the broad shoulders to take the load, and choose to fix your gaze on the Lover of your soul. He loves you so very much! He has chosen you to be His forever.

If you are tempted to throw in the towel, listen to these words from the Lord to your heart:

> So we're not giving up. How could we! Even though on the outside it often looks like things are falling apart on us, on the inside, where God is making new life, not a day goes by without His unfolding grace. (2 Corinthians 4:16 MSG)

His unfolding grace keeps on holding you up and giving you courage to continue each time you require it. God's grace is enough! It's enough for you to make it through the difficult times. It's enough to give you hope when you're disappointed. It's enough to give you vision when you've lost sight of the goal of your faith. God's unfolding grace is enough for you to live victoriously!

Papa says to you:

Don't despair. I'm still for you. My heart hasn't changed one little bit. I know you don't understand all My ways. I haven't asked you to. But one day you'll see everything the way it truly is, from My perspective. Until that time, know I am with you and I am for you. Keep on believing My good and tender heart toward you. I am everything you need. I will always be everything you need. Keep drawing into Me and keep drawing from Me. My presence will never disappoint you. My presence is everything you need. My presence is your ultimate destiny.

Chapter Reflections

- How have you seen God weave together various parts of your life's journey into a brilliant plan A for you?

- While sitting in His lap, ask your heavenly Father to show you the perceived failures in your life from His perfect perspective.

- Where do you need an upgrade in your understanding of God's ability and desire to take care of you?

- Sit with God and ask Him to give you a glimpse into the chapters that are still ahead for you in your life. While you may not see many details, be sure to notice the smile on His face when He points to the future plans He has for you! What encouragement does He have for you at the point of your journey that you're presently at? Be sure to write it down.

- Is there something about your past where you feel you've blown it so badly that God can't use you? Choose right now to receive God's forgiveness in Christ and leave that false shame and condemnation behind. Declare out loud, "I forgive myself for not being perfect. I am not disqualified! Jesus has pre-qualified me to live out my destiny."

- What is one practical step you can take towards pursuing a dream God has placed in your heart?

Chapter 6

A Lavish Father

❦

I am a loving Father, not a scary one.
You never have to be afraid when you come to Me.
All I will ever do is love and encourage you.
That's who I am and that's what I do.

Jesus loved to tell stories to make a point. In one of those stories, Jesus told a story about a father and his two sons[1] that paints a crystal-clear picture of a Father who is fully committed to His relationship with us, no matter what.

The Prodigal Father

In many Bibles, the heading added by editors over that story reads "The Prodigal Son," but nowhere in the actual text of the story are either of the sons described as prodigals. The word *prodigal* means lavishly or extravagantly wasteful. Therefore, *prodigal* has been used by Bible editors to describe the younger son, who wanted his share of the family inheritance to do with as he pleased, only to promptly waste it on out-of-control living. The "Prodigal Son" heading leads us to focus on the son's sinfulness, but Jesus told this story primarily to describe the outrageous love of the father's heart regardless of either of his sons' actions. Truly, then, this story is about the prodigal *father.* It is a picture of a father's love that is so excessive it appears to those who don't understand to be lavishly or extravagantly wasteful.

The story opens with the younger son asking his father for his portion of the family inheritance. "Dad, I have things to do, places to go, and people to see. I want to go explore the world and do what I want. I need my freedom without anyone telling me what to do. I want my part of the family wealth right now." This brazen request was totally inappropriate for that culture, a slap in the face to his father. Yet the father responds by granting the son's request and giving him a portion of the inheritance. The father is quite aware that this request may land his younger son in trouble, but his willingness to give his son the money and let him find out for himself tells us about the atmosphere of the father's house. He clearly loved his son with a love that was empowering, not controlling or oppressive. Love must be chosen in an atmosphere of freedom.

He allowed his son to make his own choices, even if they were poor ones, and to learn from them. His goal was not to protect his son from trouble. His goal was for his son to encounter what he needed to encounter to come back home. The father, in effect, was saying, "I am secure enough that I will let you do what you need to do and wait for you to return. I know the love I've poured into you will ultimately bring you back." Amazingly, the father was not even concerned with his name being dishonored.

> From the moment his son left the doorstep, his singular focus was on the eventual return of his boy.

How else could the father have seen his son coming back from a long way off unless he was constantly and intently waiting for him? But we are getting ahead of the story.

Away from his father, the son immerses himself in a world of consumers, not life-givers. Surrounded by acquaintances who want something for nothing, he's an instant hit—the life of the party because of his seemingly endless resources. Though this life of self-absorption offered so much promise from a distance, it was merely an illusion that became a prison. Eventually he's eaten alive in that culture. Since he's unplugged from his father's house, his resources are quite limited. Soon he's completely bankrupt, with no money and an empty soul to show for his disastrous escapade. He finds himself reduced to feeding pigs while he himself goes hungry.

Finally, the wayward son comes to his senses.[2] This is the pivotal point of the story. He realizes that all the allure of the world was just fool's gold and he begins to see things as they truly are.

> He realizes that everything he ever really wanted he already had in the safety of his father's house.

It dawns on him that if he'd stayed in his father's house, he would've had no need to demand his share of the inheritance because everything there was already his. He genuinely misses the love of his father and the safety of his father's house and he wants to go back home![3]

Although the son knows that home is where he belongs, his rehearsed speech is clear evidence that he has forgotten the true nature of his father's heart. Falsely believing his father to be enraged and embarrassed by his son's poor decisions, he hopes only that he can be a servant in his father's estate.

When you and I forget who we are as princes and princesses who are heirs of our Father's kingdom, we can make some very poor decisions in life. But this never changes our Father's affection for us as His children. When we beat ourselves up for our mistakes and demote ourselves to the role of a servant, even believing that it's a spiritual thing to do so, we are inadvertently agreeing with the enemy's assertion that we are good-for-nothing down-and-outs. Nothing could be further from the truth! Agreeing with the enemy's lies does nothing to bring us even one inch closer to the Father.

> Slavery is such a poor substitute for sonship! They are opposites; the one leads forcefully through fear; sonship responds fondly to Abba Father. (Romans 8:15 TMT)

The truth is that we're never separated from our Father and His consuming love for us. We sometimes *feel* separated because we have a misguided concept that sin separates us from God. While that was certainly true in the old covenant of the law, it is not true in the new covenant of grace once you've accepted the perfect sacrifice of Jesus on your behalf.

> So, what do you think? With God on our side like this, how can we lose? If God didn't hesitate to put everything on the line for us, embracing our condition and exposing himself to the worst by sending his own Son, is there anything else he wouldn't gladly and freely do for us? And who would dare tangle with God by messing with one of God's chosen? Who would dare even to point a finger? The one who died for us—who was raised to life for us!— is in the presence of God at this very moment sticking up for us. Do you think anyone is going to be able to drive a wedge between us and Christ's love for us? There is no way! Not trouble, not hard times, not hatred, not hunger, not homelessness, not bullying threats, not backstabbing, not even the worst sins listed in Scripture. (Romans 8:31–35 MSG)

This is the heart of the gospel. We have a Father who fully took upon Himself the responsibility for providing the way, in Christ, for us to be perfectly right with Him—not just when we think we're doing good, but all the time. Why would He do such a thing? In a word … *love!*

Back to the story. The son chooses to return home, and his father, who sees him from a long way off, runs to him and embraces him, unable to stop kissing him. Jesus' listeners are quite aware that this is extravagant behavior from a Jewish father to a son who, by all cultural standards, greatly dishonored his father. Yet none of that matters to the father. All that matters is that his son has returned home!

The son, still not fully believing his father's heart, tries to launch into his servanthood speech about being unworthy to be his father's son, but his father will have nothing to do with that.

> Son, don't speak such nonsense. You are my son! You will always be my son. Absolutely nothing has changed. You're going to understand my kindness and mercy in a way you never knew before. I do not judge you; I accept you and welcome you into my home and yours. That's right, you are home, my son. I have been waiting for this day. I knew it would come and here you are. Everything else is forgotten!

The father then speaks to the servants. "Quick! Bring the evidences of sonship. Dress my son in his proper attire." Immediately, the father engages in restoring the whole inheritance to his son.

Full Restoration

What transpires next is nothing short of astounding.

The first act of the father to his returning son is to put the finest robe in his house on him. The best robe in the house is the one worn by the father. The next time his son goes into the marketplace wearing his father's robe, people are going to see him coming and believe it is the father and give the son the respect due the father. This kind of extravagant love brings instant healing and strength.

Next he restores his son with a ring. The ring symbolizes the power and authority of the father. "Son, you do not have to pay for your mistakes with a prolonged absence of my power. I restore your authority to represent me." This boy, who had squandered his father's wealth in wild living, can now go about his father's business because he wears the ring of authority on his finger. Receiving that vote of confidence from his hero—his dad—instantly transforms the son.

If that weren't enough, the father completes the restoration process to his son by providing the sandals of sonship. The only people allowed to don footwear in the house were the family members. Slaves and servants went barefoot. The father was declaring in no uncertain terms that his son, despite everything he had done, was still his son and was entitled to all the rights and privileges of being his heir.

The father was saying to his servants:

> You treat him as my son. He forgot who he was out there in the influence of the world. He completely lost his perspective of who I am as his father. You follow him around and make sure he doesn't forget his robe, his shoes, and his ring of authority. You treat him like a son until he begins to live out of his own fullness of identity and confidence again, until he remembers that I have held nothing back and have set him in place as my son. And by the way—kill the fatted calf. It's time to party. My son is back!

The only thing that limits us from living in the fullness of our wealthy inheritance is our inability or unwillingness to believe the extent of our Father's benevolent heart toward us.

Our Father wants to bring us back into the reality of His atmosphere of love and acceptance and touch our hearts with the truth that everything He has is ours. Everything.

> Can you see how foolish it would be for a son to continue to live his life with a slave mentality? Your sonship qualifies you to immediately participate in all the wealth of God's inheritance which is yours because of Christ. (Galatians 4:7 TMT)

Understand that God is willing to orchestrate a famine around you through your poor choices, creating a scenario to bring you back into His presence. He doesn't do this because He's mean or manipulative, but because He loves you like crazy and knows exactly what you were created for. If you've found yourself wandering far from the love of your Father, give up your pride and come to your senses. Let Papa capture your heart once again. No more running away from the One who loves you. It's time to run back into Daddy's waiting arms!

The Robe, Ring, and Sandals Are for You

I want to encourage you to use your sanctified imagination and experience the exhilaration and relief of feeling Papa slip a robe over your shoulders, His very own robe of righteousness. Feel the security and the acceptance of this weighty, glorious robe that now envelops you as His beloved son or daughter.

> He has dressed me with the clothing of salvation and draped me in a robe of righteousness. I am like a bridegroom in his wedding suit or a bride with her jewels. (Isaiah 61:10 NLT)

This robe is our righteousness, our perfectly right standing with God provided through the precious blood of Jesus Christ. It's the garment that God covers each of us with so that when He looks at us, He only sees us washed and wholly pure. He doesn't have any remembrance of our sins.[4] The robe symbolizes our acceptability before the Father, who covers us with His approval and provides the solution in Christ for our hurts, our shame, our failures, our mistakes, and our feelings of inadequacy. As He wraps His robe around us, we become more and more like our Dad!

> And all of us, with unveiled faces, seeing the glory of the Lord as though reflected in a mirror, are being transformed into the same image from one degree of glory to another; for this comes from the Lord, the Spirit. (2 Corinthians 3:18 NRSV)

Now hold out your hand and let Him slip a ring on your finger. Go ahead—see what happens. As the ring slips over your knuckle, sense the authority that our Father and King joyfully grants to you— authority over the enemy and authority to rightly display His love and power to others. He has full confidence in what He's doing in your life so you will accurately represent His heart to others.

He looks into your eyes with extreme kindness and nods at you knowingly, giving you His full approval to be His ambassador on this earth.[5] You are His choice!

Finally, extend one foot at a time as a sandal is lovingly placed on each of them. Look again straight into the Father's affectionate eyes as He says forcefully, so it leaves an indelible imprint on your mind, "You are Mine! You have always been Mine and you will always be Mine. Never forget that! Come and share My happiness—not someday, but right now. I restore you to your rightful place as My favored child."

Some of you have never heard such words from a parent. Take it in. Believe it. This is real. If God is touching your heart right now, linger in this place with Him for a while.

Don't Be a Party-Pooper

To finish the story, there is also the matter of the older son who stays at home. The parable is not just about one lost son. The elder son is lost too. He may not have physically left his father's house like his younger brother, but his heart is just as disconnected, if not more so. Jesus wants us to hear the heart of the Father, not only for those who go off the deep end in wild, self-absorbed living, but also for those who replace the joy of living life with Papa for the drudgery of working to try to earn His approval. Neither results in the life our Father intended for us to have.

The older son hears the noise of the party that's just begun for his younger brother, but rather than experiencing gladness that his sibling has returned, he's fuming mad and refuses to come in. In much the same way as the father ran to embrace his younger son just moments before, he now leaves the party to go to his bitter older son, whom he loves equally, imploring him to come inside. Jesus is making it plain that our heavenly Father is always the One seeking us and inviting us to join in the celebration.

But the eldest son isn't going to be won over so quickly. He wants to nurse his seething soul. He rants, "This son of yours (he can't bring himself to call him "my brother") has taken what you gave him and foolishly thrown it away on prostitutes and who knows what else. He's made a fool of you, Dad! Not like me. I've done every single thing you have asked me to do. What's up with giving junior a party? Where's the accountability? Where's the probation period? When does he get the axe for what he did? Where's the justice? And where's my reward?" In his bitterness, the older son is just as far from the father's heart as the younger son was.

The kind-hearted father replies:

> Son, hear my heart. Everything I have is yours. Don't you know you can't work for what you already have? I won't let you work for it, because it's all yours. I didn't give you work to do just to keep you busy, and I certainly didn't intend for you to work for an inheritance that's my delight to give you. My joy is in being with you and having you work alongside me. I had to celebrate your brother, but I also celebrate you. Won't you come in and enjoy the feast with us?

What happened to the elder son? Did he go in? Jesus doesn't tell us. I believe each of us writes our own ending to this story. If we've been working our heads off to please God, thinking it was increasing our status with Him, resentment can cause us to stay outside. Or we can hear the joy in our Father's voice and go inside the house where it's warm and cozy and join in the party, partaking of the feast prepared for us. The choice is ours. Those stuck in legalism—thinking they can earn God's approval by what they do—become miserable, exhausted, and rigidly judgmental of others. A person can only bear this for so long before wanting to quit this entire "Christian thing" and walk away. You might hear these people say, "I tried Christianity and it didn't work." What they tried was to keep rules and be good for

God without being successful. This isn't the Father's plan. Jesus told us this story for us to know the Father's true heart, just as He knew it to be firsthand.

The apostle Paul put it this way:

> I tried keeping rules and working my head off to please God, and it didn't work. So I quit being a "law man" so that I could be God's man. (Galatians 2:19 MSG)

Notice in this story the relationship of the father to each of his sons is never broken and never even in question. At the beginning he is a father to each son, and at the end he is still a father to each son. Nothing has changed!

A Perpetual Party

When my sons, Derek and Aaron, were growing up, Suzanne and I loved planning and throwing parties for them. We'd watch them laugh as they played with their friends and see their faces light up with the delight of feeling special. And there was something exceptionally fun about watching them open a gift they really wanted but weren't sure they'd receive. You could read the expression on their faces—*What? You got this for me? Oh, yeah!* An outsider looking in might think the gift was excessive and over-the-top. But we couldn't help ourselves—and we didn't want to. That's the joy of lavishing love on your children!

Your Father in heaven loves a good party! So much so, He's the One throwing it!

When Jesus told stories to let people know what His Father was really like, He made it pretty clear that His Dad loved parties. Anyone who thinks we don't have a fun Daddy doesn't understand Him at all. When the lost sheep was found, He threw a party. When a lost coin was found, He threw a party. And when His lost son came home, even after wasting the Father's inheritance, He simply had to throw a party.

And not just a quaint little tea party, but an all-out, kill-the-fatted-calf, everybody-get-crazy fun bash!

What explanation can you give for this kind of excessiveness? The best one I can think of is that God is really, really happy and He loves to spread the joy around. And just what brings Him so much joy that He can't help Himself and can't keep it to Himself? I believe deep down inside of you, you already know the answer. *You* do! You bring Him intense joy. You bring him so much joy that He looks for ways to lavish His love on you.

He looks for gifts to give you that are over-the-top and excessive. Not because He has to (that wouldn't be any fun), but because He wants to. That's what love does.

You are the one God must have. One glance from you turns His heart inside out. The one He is lovesick for is you. And since the price has been paid for in full by Jesus on the cross to have you as His very own forever, He chooses to throw a perpetual party!

> Celebrate God, the Father of our Boss, Jesus the Liberator. 'Cause of our connection with the Liberator, God's poured out so much of heaven's good stuff that our belly laughs are fuller, longer, stronger than ever before. Way back, before the cosmos was called to attention out of nothing, God let the Liberator pick us out to be His special people, fully acquitted and loved! What God always wanted, what He craved for was for us to fulfill our destiny—to be adopted into His family through our links with Jesus the Liberator. And He loves His Son so much He just piles on the dazzling freebies and we're left speechless—except for making sure that God gets all the credit for everything we've got. Our Jesus-link sparks off all of God's over-the-top generosity. If it wasn't for His wisdom in knowing

how we tick, you'd think he was spoiling us with all these bonuses! (Ephesians 1:3–6 *The Word on the Street*)

Raw Grace

Our Father's arms are big enough to embrace the one wandering into sinful choices as well as the one caught in a web of trying to measure up by right actions. Astoundingly, neither one is disqualified from their inheritance. Both receive the Father's love and acceptance. This is His willful and joyful response of grace and mercy every single day of our lives.

We, on the other hand, have a tendency to judge people even though our Father chooses to hold absolutely nothing against us. If we're not careful, we can judge people we deem to be engaged in sinful living, and we can also fall into the trap of judging people who are still locked into religious legalism of rule-keeping. Instead, we should take our lead from our Father, who says to both, "Come here. Come in closer still. Know the goodness of My heart. The party is for you! As you come to know and believe My heart for you, you will be true to who I have created you to be."

Papa continually extends His hand and invites all of His children into His good and perfect plan for their lives, even in the midst of our poor choices.

Grace in its most raw and pure form, unmarred by religion's death grip, almost sounds wrong or too good to be true. But the more you hear the truth of genuine grace, the more you are set free to enjoy your Papa who so enjoys you!

In a wonderful book called *The Ragamuffin Gospel*, author Brennan Manning says:

"Justification by grace through faith" is the theologian's learned phrase for what Chesterton once called, "the furious love of God!" He is not moody or capricious; He knows no seasons of change. He has a single relentless stance toward us: He loves us. He is the only God man has ever heard of who loves sinners. False gods—the gods of human manufacturing—despise sinners, but the Father of Jesus loves all, no matter what they do. But of course this is almost too incredible for us to accept. Nevertheless, the central affirmation of the Reformation stands: through no merit of ours, but by His mercy, we have been restored to a right relationship with God through the life, death, and resurrection of His beloved Son! This is the Good News, the gospel of grace![6]

Robert Capon puts the historical discovery of grace in a compelling light:

The Reformation was a time when men went blind, staggering drunk because they had discovered, in the dusty basement of late medievalism, a whole cellar full of fifteen-hundred-year-old, two-hundred proof Grace— bottle after bottle of pure distillate of Scripture, one sip of which would convince anyone that God saves us single-handedly. The word of the Gospel—after all those centuries of trying to lift yourself into heaven by worrying about the perfection of your bootstraps—suddenly turned out to be a flat announcement that the saved were home before they started. Grace has to be drunk straight: no water, no ice, and certainly no ginger ale; neither goodness, nor badness, nor the flowers that bloom in the spring of super spirituality could be allowed to enter into the case.[7]

Too many Christians are not living in the freedom that was purchased for them at such an extreme cost. They are depressed, believing the lie that God is mad at them because they're not getting it just right. That's not the way it's supposed to be and it's certainly not the way it has to be.

We have a Father who adores us, a Savior who has done everything to set us free, and the Holy Spirit, who's been given to us to live it out. Wow! That about takes care of everything!

Our part is to actually believe God's grace-plan is that good and to live accordingly as radical lovers of this amazingly lavish Dad.

Your Father says to you:

> You are welcome in My house, My child. I have a place just for you. You're not a servant or a slave. You're My son/daughter and you get to eat the feast I've prepared for you. I gladly sit with you, My beloved. Come into My rest. Lay your head on My chest. Shhhh … Listen to My heartbeat. Listen. It beats for you!

This would be a great time to stop and do just as Papa is encouraging you to do. If you sense within you that He is telling you something about His heart for you, take the time to write it down in a journal.

Chapter Reflections

- Where in your life in the past or present do you identify with the younger son who forgot who he was?

- Where in your life in the past or present do you identify with the older son who tried to earn what was already his?

- If you need to remember who you are as a true son or daughter, stand up where you are. Really. Go ahead and stand up. Ask Papa to place His royal robe over your shoulders. Hold out your hand and allow Him to place His ring of authority on your finger. Finally, put forward one foot and then the other to slip into the sandals of sonship and daughtership. Bask in the truth that you fully belong in your Father's house!

- Will you accept the Father's invitation to join His party? What does a party kingdom-style look like?
- How does grace in its most raw and real form feel to you? If it feels good, revel in it some more. If it feels a little uncomfortable at first, ask God to help you release any religious baggage you may have picked up along the way.

SECTION TWO

༄

Daring to Believe
It's True

Choosing to Embark Upon the Journey

of a Lifetime

Chapter 7

Revealing the Father's True Heart

I want you to enjoy Me as I really am.
Look at Jesus, who perfectly represented Me on this earth.
Then look at Me again and see the softness in My eyes.
I'm much, much better than you know.
Come in closer still!

Recently, after feeling terribly misunderstood by someone, I started complaining to God. (I'm just being honest!) *Papa, why, when I'm just trying to help people, do they turn it around somehow and question my heart? I've loved them and cared for them, but I feel like I'm on trial for something I didn't do.*

It's good to talk with God about anything and everything, but you won't often get the response you were expecting. Do you know what I heard from God? He said to me, *I know exactly how you feel. You've done that to Me many times.*

What? I shot back in disbelief. But quickly I knew He was right.

He went on, *I'm not upset with you, Son, but My heart is misunderstood by My children continuously. Because they don't know the depth of My heart for them and because they cannot comprehend the nature of My all-consuming love that motivates everything I do, they build cases against Me and make accusations about My character that have nothing at all in common with My true nature.*

I began to feel a fraction of God's pain of being so misunderstood by the very ones who are the central focus of His affection.

Lord, I'm so sorry.

He responded:

> I have a plan woven throughout history of bringing the true revelation of who I am to all of My children around the world. I picked a time in history to make Myself completely visible through My beloved Son, Jesus. I've now placed My very own Spirit within those who accept the perfect sacrifice of My Son on their behalf and they, too, are carriers of My glory. My glory is My nature, My character. By My Spirit, I am convincing My children of My genuine love—and the more they perceive My heart correctly, the more accurately they are taking it to every corner of the world.

The author of the book of Hebrews explains the Father's perfect plan:

> Throughout ancient times God spoke in many fragments and glimpses of prophetic thought to our fathers. Now, the sum total of His conversation with man has finally culminated in a son; He is the official heir of all things; He is, after all, the author of the ages. In Him everything finds its destiny. We have our beginning and our being in Him. He is the force of the universe that sustains everything that is by His eternal utterance, the INCARNATION! He makes the glory of God visible in radiant reflection; He gives stature to the character and person of God in human form. This powerful final utterance of God is the vehicle that carries the weight of the universe. He is the central theme of everything that

exists. The content of His message celebrates the fact that God took it upon Himself to successfully purge and acquit mankind. Jesus is now His right hand of power, seated in the boundless measure of His majesty. He occupies the highest seat of authority there representing our innocence. (Hebrews 1:1–3 TMT)

The Perfect Representation

Our heavenly Father has been terribly misunderstood throughout history. There have always been individuals who've grasped His extreme goodness, but unfortunately most people have kept their distance from Him out of fear.

The Israelites in the time of Moses, for example, didn't want to meet with God because they didn't truly believe His intentions were for their best. They were petrified and wanted Moses to go and meet with God in their place. They said, "Don't let God speak to us or we'll die. We'll do whatever God tells you, Moses."[1]

When Moses came back from meeting with God, the radiance on his face scared the people instead of causing them to want a similar experience with God for themselves.[2] It truly broke the Father's heart that the people He called to be His very own were afraid of Him and didn't trust Him. Our Father has always wanted to be with His children. Always!

Later in history the Israelites demanded a king.[3] Once again, the Father was crushed. His wounded heart cried out:

I would be your king if only you saw My true heart for you. But because you want a human king and because I love you, I will grant your request. Know that My heart is to be your provider, your lover, your friend, and your king. I am the Good Shepherd, and I will lay down My life for you. One day I will send My Son, who will clearly demonstrate My true heart for you. He will become the King of all kings, and the only king you will ever need.

Even to this day, there still persists in many a belief that the Father is scary, and they only want to interact with Jesus. They hold on to a false perception that Jesus and the Father have very divergent natures. They would say, "Jesus I like. He's feels safe. But I'm not so sure about the Father. Isn't He the angry, vengeful One? You know, the One who is ticked off at me and is waiting to punish me?"

They somehow hold to a belief that a wrathful Father is poised to strike them down, while Jesus stands in between, pleading on their behalf, "Noooo, Dad! Don't wipe them off the face of the earth. Don't do it! I love them."

This scenario is laughable. Jesus plainly stated, "Anyone who has seen Me, has seen My Father,"[4] and, "I only do what I see My Father doing."[5]

So if we want a clearer picture of our Father, we need to look even more intently at Jesus. And the more we explore the genuine heart of Jesus and of His Father, who is our Father, we realize they are of the very same essence and nature, exactly as Jesus Himself said: "I and the Father are one."[6]

When Jesus was sent to show us the Father, He didn't reveal a brand-new God with a new-and-improved personality. He came to show us the eternally existent One, "the Father of celestial lights in whom there is no variation or shadow of change."[7]

Jesus became a man—God with skin on—to clear up centuries of errant understandings of God's character. Jesus is the Father's ultimate and supreme statement of His abundant love for us.

Jesus is proof-positive of Papa's unmerited favor toward us, His extreme graciousness that sustains us, and His unparalleled goodness that continually showers us with His blessings.

Through Jesus, the Father has proven to each of us:

> You are My greatest treasure. You are worth everything to Me. I absolutely must have you as My very own forever and ever. I have left *nothing* to chance. By My will, Jesus

took upon Himself every hideous thing that would ever try to come between you and Me. At the conclusion of His sacrificial death for you on the cross, I tore the veil around the Holy of Holies, which was a symbol of separation, as though it were a piece of frail tissue paper. And as I did so, I screamed, "NO MORE!"

No more separation! No more division! No more estrangement, disconnection, or indifference! All has been made right. Never again will My children be at odds with Me. Complete and total reconciliation has been restored. Never do you need to tiptoe into My Presence—I urge you to run with reckless abandon, knocking things over on your way if you must. Come and leap into My waiting arms of love and let's laugh and enjoy life together. *This* is My heart.

For all who have misunderstood Me, I sent My Son, Jesus, to perfectly display My unchanging character of love. Please believe Me when I tell you this love is yours forever!

And just for the record, God doesn't love you because of Jesus. He loves you because of *you*.

He loves you in the very same way and with the same intensity that He loves His Son, Jesus. Jesus is the proof of just how far that love would go to make sure you would live with Him forever.

God Is After Lovers

Let's look deeper into the true heart of the Father that Jesus came to reveal. As you gain a clearer perspective of how wonderful our Father is, you'll have the eyes to see His nature of love throughout the Bible. One clear evidence of His tender heart toward us is in the book of Hosea, found in the Old Testament.

Though this Scripture was written to the nation of Israel, the unchanging nature of His precious promises are for us as well, because of our lineage through our Messiah, Jesus.[8] In other words, we get to grab these promises as our very own. This particular passage has been a huge comfort to me, especially through challenging seasons of my life:

> But look, I am going to allure her and lead her into the desert and speak to her heart. There I shall give her back her vineyards and make the Vale of Achor [the Valley of Misfortune] a gateway of hope. There she will respond as when she was young, as on the day when she came up from Egypt. When that day comes—declares Yahweh—you will call me, "My Husband," no more will you call me "My Master." (Hosea 2:14–16 NJB, words in brackets added)

There are times in our lives when we are in what can only be described as a dry and barren place. We may have made certain choices that put us there, or we may have done nothing whatsoever to cause it. Nevertheless, God's promise to us is this:

> When you find yourself in a dry, arid place in life, know that I will not leave you there, because I have a much greater plan for you, My beloved. I will speak tenderly to your heart from the abundance of My great affection for you. When that happens, I will restore the fruitfulness in your life. That means what you were born to release to this world will most certainly happen. I will flip around your circumstances and turn what appears to be a negative into a breathtaking positive!

> As you see My kindness, you will respond again, just like you did when I first set you free from your sinful past and I became your first love.[9] Even though you have loved Me, somewhere along the way our relationship was reduced to that of master-servant. That's not okay with Me. That's not what I'm after.

I've always wanted one thing: a love relationship with those whowantMeinreturn.I'mbreathingfreshlifeintoyourheart, allowingyou to see Me as your Husband who cares for you in love. I'm not a master who would manipulate you with fear and intimidation.

This is consistent with what Jesus taught. He said, "I shall no longer call you servants, because a servant does not know his master's business. I call you friends because I have made known to you everything I have learned from My Father."[10]

In total agreement with the Father, Jesus is saying: "Servanthood is a good quality in the Christian life, but relationally our Father desires lovers. Don't settle for servanthood as the basis of your relationship with Him—you'll miss out on all the treasures that mutual love has to offer."

It will no longer be a one-sided affair. I will be your God and you will be My people, not by force but by mutual desire. (Hebrews 8:10 TMT)

Heidi Baker, an amazing daughter of the King who is being used to usher in the kingdom of heaven in Mozambique, Africa, described the transition in her life from servant to lover like this:

The Lord asked her, "Heidi, what would you like to do?"

Her response was "Lord, I want to do whatever You ask me to do." While this sounds very spiritual, and there's actually a time and place for this kind of response, the Lord was looking for something more specific.

He continued, "I know you'll do whatever I ask, but what do you want to do, Heidi?"

She replied, "Well, what I really want to do is take care of the widows and orphans in Mozambique."

The Lord said to her, "Good! That's what I want to do too. Let's do that together."

Part of our journey is learning to yield to the Lord because we trust He genuinely has our best interests in mind at all times.

> The more we understand His heart and the more our
> new nature in Christ becomes our natural response in life,
> the more we realize our Papa intends for us to be in
> a co-laboring role with Him as lovers and friends
> who enjoy doing things together.

I can understand this much more clearly as I think about my relationship with my amazing wife, Suzanne. If I were to always wait for her to tell me what to do, then compliantly respond, "Yes, dear … Yes, dear … Yes, dear," that would be a sad relationship. If Suzanne were to say, "Let's do something together," and my only response was, "We'll do whatever you want to do," she'd soon come to the conclusion that she married a mindless robot when what she desires is real relationship. Of course, there are times when I sincerely want to let Suzanne know that what she wants to do is important to me. But if that were my only dialogue with her, there would be no mutual joy in that relationship, no experiencing life together.

Lovers of God want to please God, not because of fear or intimidation or any other motivation that doesn't last. Lovers of God want to please Him because that's what lovers naturally do. Since God has eliminated what stood in the way of our intimacy with Him—especially guilt, condemnation and shame—we have been given freedom and an invitation to experience greater levels of closeness with Him. We then want to heed the promptings of the Holy Spirit so that nothing hinders that intimacy in any way. The presence of God feels so good it entices us to want more.

This is the one true and lasting motivation that causes us to say yes to all the promptings of the Holy Spirit to live in the fullness of our new nature and to walk away from our old, dead life of sin. Once you've tasted the goodness of the Lord, nothing else compares! You have your Father's invitation right now to move in even deeper.

Direct Access to the Father

Your Father has a soft place in His heart just for you that gives you direct access to Him as an insider.

> Entering into the fullness of Christ is not something you figure out or achieve. It's not a matter of being circumcised or keeping a long list of laws. No, you're already in—insiders—not through some initiation rite but rather through what Christ has already gone through for you, destroying the power of sin. (Colossians 2:11–12 MSG)

During the American Civil War, a Union Army soldier who had lost his father and his brother in the war went to Washington DC to speak with President Lincoln to ask for an exemption from military service to help his mother and sister on their farm. However, upon arriving at the White House, he was told that he could not see the President because Mr. Lincoln was too busy with the details of the war. Distraught, he sat on a nearby bench when a young boy approached him and asked, "What's wrong, soldier?" The soldier poured his heart out to the boy about his situation.

The little boy took the soldier by the hand and led him around to the back of the White House. They went through the back door, past the guards, past all the generals and the high-ranking government officials until they got to the President's office itself. The little boy didn't even knock on the door but just opened it and walked in. There was President Lincoln with his Secretary of State, looking over battle plans on the desk. President Lincoln looked up and asked, "What can I do for you, Todd?"

Todd happened to be President Lincoln's son, and he said, "Daddy, this soldier needs to talk to you." Right then and there the soldier had a chance to share his story with the President and was exempted from military service due to the hardship his family was under.[11]

Because of Jesus, we have been given the breathtaking right to come straight to our Father, who, unlike President Lincoln, always has time for us.

> Papa not only has all of the solutions and resources
> to provide for what we need, but He especially loves
> it when we just want a hug and to be near him.

He says, "Oh, *that* I love most of all! Come in closer."

We don't come to Him once we think we have our act together or when we think we are clean enough or good enough. If that were the case, we would all still be waiting outside. No, we have a Daddy who adores us so much He devised a plan—that Jesus carried out—so we could come to Him clean and perfect as His precious children, all of the time!

> For by a single offering, Christ has perfected for all time those who are sanctified." (Hebrews 10:14 RSV)

> So, friends, we can now—without hesitation—walk right up to God, into "the Holy Place." Jesus has cleared the way by the blood of His sacrifice, acting as our priest before God. The "curtain" into God's presence is Christ's body. So let's do it—full of belief, confident that we're presentable inside and out. (Hebrews 10:19–22 MSG)

> Let us, then, have no fear in approaching the throne of grace to receive mercy and to find grace when we are in need of help. (Hebrews 4:16 NJB)

Your Daddy in heaven says to you:

> Child, how about that hug? In My arms you can let Me know whatever is troubling you, but in My presence you may just forget those troubles, because I'm here to love on you and to reassure you that I know how to take care of you!

Hanging Out with the Father

Our Father loves spending time with us—so much so that He has determined never to be apart from us. On the flip side, I often hear people express their feelings of inadequacy in the amount of time and quality of time that they are spending with God. They are either lamenting the past days, weeks, or months when they haven't spent enough time with God, or they are determining a new course of action in the days to come. ("Tomorrow, I'll get up earlier to spend time with God.") Both responses overlook the obvious choice of spending time with God *right now!*

> Spending time with Papa right now doesn't mean putting aside everything else you were planning to do today. It's simply enjoying the pleasure of being with Him moment by moment throughout your day.

Bemoaning the past is truly wasted energy, mainly because it fixes all of your attention on your own efforts and performance (or rather, your *lack* of performance). Looking at your own past efforts and determining to improve them in some sort of self-help program isn't what God is after. He's after lovers, and true lovers can't help gazing at each other and enjoying each other throughout the day. It's what lovers do! As long as spending time with your Father is relegated to checking something off of your to-do list for the day, you'll never enjoy sweet intimacy with Him the way you were born to. But God is saying to you:

> Yoo-hoo! I'm right here. Stop looking at what you perceive to be your failures and look back at Me. I'm the one with a twinkle in My eye that sparkles because of you. Look at My gaze. There you go! That's much better.

Simply talk with Him … right now. Invite Him into whatever you are doing at this very moment.

Everything is better when it's shared with someone you love, right?

Papa begins a dialogue with you. *What'cha doing?*

You respond, *Nothin' much, really. It's not that important.*

To which He replies, *Whatever you're doing is very important to Me, and I just like being with you. Can we do it together?*

Lovers don't always have to be talking. It's enough just to be near each other while you're doing whatever it is you're doing.

But after a time God says, *Do you want to know what I like doing?*

You stop for a moment, because it never really dawned on you that you could ask and find out what God wants to do.

With a warm smile on His face He says to you ...

I will let you finish this story and let Papa tell you what it is He likes doing as you spend time with Him right now, discovering the true heart of your Father.

If you aren't perceiving His gentle communication with you just yet, go easy on yourself. Keep asking for and expecting His response. He's communicating with you all the time, but almost never in an audible way. This is a Spirit-to-spirit encounter, which means it's something you sense from deep within. Instead of dismissing this as your own thoughts, you will begin to understand that God is feeding you sweet truths from His heart to yours.

"I am my beloved's and He is mine!" (Song of Songs 2:16 NIV)

Chapter Reflections

- Talk with God about where you have misunderstood His heart. Give Him the opportunity to share His heart with you the way it truly is.

- Can you see places in your life where you have been okay with simply being God's servant? Accept His invitation to encounter Him as a friend and as a lover. How will that change the way you live?
- How does the truth "lovers of God want to please Him" help you to understand how intimacy and holiness are directly connected?
- What do you choose to do with your direct access to the Father?

Chapter 8

The New Covenant of Grace—Too Good to Be True?

❦

I must have you with Me for all eternity,
so I will do for you what you couldn't do for yourself in a million
years.
Of this, you can be certain!

You can't truly appreciate and enjoy the Father's love apart from gaining an understanding of the new covenant of grace. And the new covenant of grace is void of any meaning apart from Jesus and what He accomplished for us on the cross. Our Father's grace plan is so astoundingly, outrageously good, it is nearly impossible for us to believe it the way is actually is. I say *nearly* because God has placed His Spirit in us to be sure we have a tutor to help us get it right!

The new covenant of grace guarantees that everything I said about the Father's heart for you in the first seven chapters of this book is true for *you*.

A Brief History of Covenant

A covenant is a contractual agreement or a promise with an iron-clad guarantee it's going to be fulfilled.

God made a covenant with Abraham that He would bless those who bless him, curse those who curse him, and make his descendants more numerous than the stars they could count in the sky.[1] That promise is still being fulfilled to this day.[2] To seal that covenant, God did something fascinating. He had Abraham split several animals in half and place each half opposite the other, creating a path down the middle. This was an ancient covenantal ritual, with both parties passing between the parts of the slaughtered animals, calling down on themselves the fate of those animals should they violate the agreement. (Pretty serious stuff!) But in this covenant God made with Abraham, He Himself was the only one walking between the animals' pieces, symbolized by a flaming torch passing through the middle.[3]

By this act, God was saying to Abraham, "This is a one-sided covenant because it's My choice to bless you. And I will make sure it happens. That's just the way it is, Abraham. I'm God and I will do it!" And because Abraham chose to believe God would keep His promise, he was declared right before God. [4] Notice he wasn't declared right with God because of how good a man he was, but simply because he said yes to God's goodness—God's choice to bless him.

Of all the people on the earth in his day, what made Abraham so special to receive a deal like this from God? Nothing, really. He didn't earn the blessing with something he did.

> Abraham was God's choice because he was God's choice, and that's what made him so special.

That's the same reason you are so special, by the way.

Later, God entered into a very different covenant with the nation of Israel (which we refer to as the old covenant) through a man named Moses. Whereas the first covenant with Abraham was a prelude, foreshadowing the grace covenant we now enjoy in Christ, this covenant with Israel was a crystal-clear picture of why a Messiah was needed to save us and set us free. Everything about the old covenant was a setup, pointing ahead toward the eventual arrival of the God-man, Christ Jesus.

After Moses came down Mount Sinai with the Ten Commandments, God made a covenant with the people of Israel. Boiled down, it was essentially this: "You will be My people and I will be your God. I offer you a blessing and a curse—a blessing if you obey all the laws I have laid out before you, and a curse if you disobey."[5]

Unlike the covenant with Abraham, this covenant was a two-way deal. Both sides agreed to the promise and both sides had to keep to their agreement. God was aware that Israel couldn't keep their end of the bargain (due to the entity called sin that entered the human race with Adam's fall), so He allowed for a sacrificial system in which the high priest would offer an atoning sacrifice once a year for the sins of the people. Because of the innate sense of God's justice placed within each person created in His image, the need for somebody to have to pay for wrongdoings was alleviated through this sacrificial system. The weight of the guilt and shame that had built up over a year's time from not being able to perfectly keep the Law was also lightened, at least temporarily. The sacrificial animals chosen for this once-a-year ritual of release had to be perfect, spotless, and blameless. It was a Band-Aid until the promised Savior would come to do something about the sin problem permanently.

> You know that the price of your ransom from the futile way of life handed down from your ancestors was paid, not in anything perishable like silver or gold, but in precious blood as of a blameless and spotless lamb, Christ. (1 Peter 1:18–19 NJB)

In heaven they are singing this new song to the risen Savior, Jesus:

> You are worthy to take the scroll and to break its seals, because You were sacrificed, and with Your blood You bought people for God of every race, language, people and nation and made

them a line of kings and priests for God, to rule the world. (Revelation 5:9–10 NJB)

> The old covenant made humankind's complete in-ability to help or save ourselves painfully obvious, thereby pointing us to our desperate need for a Savior to do for us what we could not do for ourselves.

Jesus came to put the final nail in the coffin of the old covenant and to inaugurate the new covenant of grace in its place. There was just one problem. In order for the old covenant to end, somebody was going to have to die.

That ritualistic ceremony of the two parties walking between the dead animals, saying, "May this happen to me if I don't keep my end of the bargain," had to be kept. And this time the covenant was between both parties, not a unilateral agreement on God's part alone. So either the nation of Israel or God Himself would have to die. Killing the "apple of His eye," Israel, was unthinkable, so God came to earth in the form of a man, Jesus. And God died.

But to keep Israel's end of the bargain so that the nation of His beloved people would not also have to die, this one Man, Jesus, lived His life on earth perfectly keeping every minute detail of the entirety of the Mosaic Law, so that with His last breath on the cross, He could rightfully say, "It is finished!"[6]

This is why Jesus said, "I have not come to abolish the Law, but to fulfill it."[7] Some mistakenly think Jesus is instructing us to continue living by the Law. But He came to do what no human being could do or would ever be able to do. The Law's singular purpose is to let us know that we're law-breakers so we would recognize our need for a Savior.[8] Once we find Jesus, the Law has fulfilled its purpose and we are home free, with a brand-new nature, living in a whole new kingdom!

Glimpses of Glory

The new covenant of grace was described by the prophets in the Bible many generations before it would be activated at Jesus' death on the cross. We're now living in the glorious days of which they only saw glimpses.

God spoke through the prophet Ezekiel describing the coming new covenant. (Notice how grace is *all* God's work.)

> I shall pour clean water over you and you will be cleansed; I shall cleanse you of all your filth and of all your foul idols. I shall give you a new heart, and put a new spirit in you; I shall remove the heart of stone from your bodies and give you a heart of flesh instead. … You will be My people and I will be your God. (Ezekiel 36:25–27 NJB)

That phrase "heart of flesh" means a heart that is responsive and sensitive to the touch of God. And that's exactly what He's placed inside of us in the new covenant. We're living in a time when Papa is activating that sensitive, responsive heart in a dynamic way. He's applying the paddles and shocking our hearts into expansive life! He's exhaling His warm breath over any cold places of our hearts to activate every bit of the love that's inside us.

God spoke through Jeremiah, giving this glance into the new covenant:

> Within them I shall plant my Law, writing it on their hearts. Then I shall be their God and they will be my people. There will be no further need for everyone to teach neighbor or brother, saying, 'Learn to know Yahweh!' No, they will all know me, from the least to the greatest, Yahweh declares, since I shall forgive their guilt and nevermore call their sins to mind. (Jeremiah 31:31–34 NJB)

In the new covenant, all of us get to know the Lord for ourselves because there is no more guilt and shame to get in the way of our intimate connection with our Father.

This, then, is the new covenant in a nutshell: God, by His choice alone, has determined to do for us what we could never do for ourselves in a million years. He has destroyed the curse of death and sin that stood against us and separated us from Him. Jesus' perfect sacrifice for us on the cross has permanently made us right with God. So that we will accurately represent God on this earth, He has put His Holy Spirit within us to continuously remind us of who we really are—our Father's cherished and favored children, who have been given His power and authority to expand His kingdom of love and grace throughout the earth.

Astounding Details of the New Covenant

As we've seen, the transition from the old covenant to the new covenant happened precisely at Jesus' death.

> Like a will that takes effect when someone dies, the New Covenant was put into action at Jesus' death. His death marked the transition from the old plan to the new one, canceling the old obligations and accompanying sins, and summoning the heirs to receive the eternal inheritance that was promised them. Jesus brought together God and His people in this new way. (Hebrews 9:16–17 MSG)

At the exact moment of Jesus' death, the old covenant was rendered null and void, and the new covenant gloriously burst into existence!

Simultaneously, the thick temple curtain that had been the symbol of the separation of God and humankind was torn right down the middle.[9] Jesus broke the curse of sin that separated us from our heavenly Father. He took it all on the cross for our sakes, and then took it all with Him to the grave, so it would never be seen or heard from again.

The new covenant of grace was made between the Father and His Son, Jesus. That makes God the sole maker and keeper of the covenant, just as in His covenant with Abraham. Picture the Father saying to Jesus, "Son, I love You with all My heart. I love all of My children and I want them with Me forever. Will You fulfill the Law perfectly and die their death so that all of us can be together?"

And Jesus responds, "Yes, Father! I love You, and I'll do this so we can all be together." The covenant was truly an eternal love agreement between Father and Son.

So then, where do we come into the picture? One of the mysteries of the new covenant is how, at the moment your eyes are opened to see who Jesus is as the Son of God and what He has done to set you free as your Savior, your "yes" to Him makes you one with Him. Being one with Jesus, who transcends time, means you are joined with Him in His past, present, and future. That puts you smack dab in the middle of this forever love covenant between Father and Son!

If you want in on this love covenant and you've never said yes to Jesus' death on your behalf, it's most certainly time to do so! You enter in by faith, and faith is believing that God wants you and took care of the sin problem that would separate you from Him forever. You might say something like this to Papa God:

> I need You and I want in. I believe You love me. I admit that I haven't been able to keep the law perfectly. I can't. I need a Savior! I need Jesus! I believe Jesus is Your Son and I believe You wanted me so much You took care of the entire sin-separation problem so I could approach You without fear and return Your love with my own for You. I accept your complete forgiveness. I agree that because of Jesus' death on my behalf, I'm washed and pure before You. I receive the gift of Your Spirit, making me a brand-new creation. I'm ready to start living life with Your Spirit inside me, giving me a love for people that I've always wanted but didn't seem to have. I want to know and experience who You are as my loving heavenly Father. I want to know

the vastness of Your love for me. I want to know You, too, Jesus. I want to know what kind of love You have for me that would willingly lead You to the cross in my place. I also want to know You, Holy Spirit. You have been given to me as a gift to help me and give me astoundingly wise counsel every day of my life. You are truly Someone I need in my corner. Immerse me in Your power. I'm realizing I'm alive to experience and enjoy Your presence, Lord. The rest of my life will come into alignment and focus as You lead me deeper into Your heart, and I finally allow myself to believe how good You really are. Let's live this life together from now on.

Write this decision down in a journal with a date on it. It's your new birthday! Oh, you still get to keep your natural birthday, celebrating the day you entered this world. But this is your spiritual birthday, when you truly became alive to why you're here.

You'll never be the same again, because God's been waiting for this moment to take up residence in you, loving you from the inside out!

Your oneness with Christ is a supernatural event. A divine transaction takes place. Everything that's Christ's is now yours. The old you, with the accompanying sin nature, has died with Him on the cross and has been buried with Him in the tomb.[10] The new you is already raised to new life with Christ, where you are seated with Him in the heavens.[11] Just by believing in Him, you are born from above—a brand-new being—your spirit and His connected inseparably. You have a brand-new nature—one nature. It is *in Christ!*

> Therefore, if anyone is in Christ, that person is a new creation; the old has gone, the new has come! (2 Corinthians 5:17 NIV)

> Anyone united with the Messiah gets a fresh start, is created
> new. The old life is gone, a new life burgeons! Look at it!
> (2 Corinthians 5:17 MSG)

The entity called sin that hung like a thousand-pound albatross around our necks because of Adam's disobedience in the garden was completely disarmed by Christ. That blight that made obedience to the old covenant impossible to keep was dealt a death blow by our mighty Savior.

Here's the problem and God's new covenant answer explained in Scripture:

> Herein is the extremity of God's love gift: Humankind
> was rotten to the core when Christ died their death. ...
> Our hostility towards God did not reduce His love for
> us; He saw equal value in us when He exchanged the life
> of His Son for ours. Now that the act of reconciliation is
> complete, His life in us saves us from the guttermost to
> the uttermost. ... One man opened the door to sin, sin
> introduced (spiritual) death; both sin and (spiritual) death
> had a global impact, no one escaped its tyranny. ... The
> only similarity in the comparison between the offense
> and the gift is that both Adam and Christ represent the
> masses—their single action therefore bears universal
> consequence. However, the difference in the effect is vast;
> one leads to (spiritual) death, the other to limitless life. ...
> The conclusion is clear: it took just one offense to condemn
> humankind; one act of righteousness declares the same
> humankind innocent. (Romans 5:8–18 TMT)

Here is that final verse, Romans 5:18, in the New Jerusalem Bible:

> One man's offence brought condemnation on all humanity;
> and one man's good act has brought justification and life to
> all humanity.

Let's take a closer look at that word *justification*, which is a hugely important aspect of the new covenant. Forgiveness we can somewhat comprehend—that our hatred and animosity toward God that led to the death of Christ on the cross was not held against us because of Papa's merciful heart. Justification, however, goes a major step beyond that. Justification says you have already been tried and found "not guilty" because there is no shred of evidence against you.

> The judge has reviewed the case against you and thrown in out of court, never to be reviewed again, because there is zero evidence to convict you of any crime. You've been acquitted!

> God has identified us; who can disqualify us? No one can point a finger; He justified us. What further ground can there possibly be to condemn man? Christ died—this cannot be undone! His resurrection cannot be wished away. He occupies the highest seat of authority at the right hand of God in our favor. (Romans 8:33–34 TMT)

It's time, once and for all, for the Church—those who believe in the saving sacrifice of Jesus on their behalf—to move past a fear-based life of wondering if we will make it into our Father's heavenly kingdom. We're already in! We're wasting precious days and years of our lives being fearful of something that Jesus already took care of for us. Fear keeps us in total bondage, never fully stepping out to be the amazing sons and daughters of the King we truly are.

The moment you said yes to Jesus, you became one with Him. You are already seated with him in heaven. That's not made-up stuff—that's the real deal!

> At some point we are going to have to trust the goodness of our Father, who took it fully upon Himself to both make and keep the most outrageous promises this world has ever known.

Just how complete was Christ's sacrifice?

> As it was by one man that death came, so through one man has come the resurrection of the dead. Just as all die in Adam, so in Christ all will be brought to life. (1 Corinthians 15:21–22 NJB)

> For there is only one God, and there is only one mediator between God and humanity, himself a human being, Christ Jesus, who offered himself as a ransom for all. (1 Timothy 2:5–6 NJB)

> You see, God's grace has been revealed to save the whole human race. (Titus 2:11 NJB)

The Judge's Verdict: Not Guilty!

Here's a view of the new covenant I've been describing from heaven's perspective.

The archangel Michael stands and shouts:

> Hear ye, hear ye! From the highest court in heaven, Yahweh, our Maker, Creator, Sustainer, and the Father from whom all fathers derive their name, gives His final verdict, never to be overturned throughout eternity.

The thunderous voice of the Ancient of Days, our heavenly Father, declares with finality:

> I have found My Son, Jesus, to be perfect in every way and thereby He has perfectly fulfilled in every minute detail the old covenant Law. Because Jesus has fulfilled man's part of the bargain for all humanity, I will forever fulfill

My part of blessing you and not cursing you. My favor will follow you all the days of your life.

Therefore, for the sake of My Son, who perfectly represented My heart toward all I've made, My judgment upon all of humanity is:

"Not Guilty!"

Here the gavel slams to the bench with an authoritative and definitive exclamation point that reverberates through space and time—past, present, and future.

Yahweh continues emphatically:

The old and inferior covenant, which was destined to pass away, was created "until death do us part." The part of My eternal triune existence who is Jesus came to the earth in human form ... and died. Upon His death, the old covenant became obsolete, and for those who are in Christ, it has completely passed away—forever finished. In its place stands a new covenant of grace for all time to come.

My decision is final and eternal!

Because this all sounds too good to be true, here is the Father's verdict through several Scriptures:

As it is, [Jesus] has been given a ministry as far superior as is the covenant of which he is the mediator, which is founded on better promises. If that first covenant had been faultless, there would have been no room for a second one to replace it. And in fact God does find fault with them; he says: Look, the days are coming, the Lord declares, when I will make a new covenant with the House of Israel and the House of Judah, but not a covenant like the one I made with their ancestors the day I took them by the hand to bring them out of Egypt, which covenant of mine they broke, and I too abandoned them, the Lord declares.

No, this is the covenant I will make with the House of Israel, when those days have come, the Lord declares: In their minds I shall plant My laws, writing them on their hearts. Then I shall be their God, and they shall be my people. There will be no further need for each to teach his neighbour, and each his brother, saying "Learn to know the Lord!" No, they will all know me, from the least to the greatest, since I shall forgive their guilt and never more call their sins to mind. By speaking of a new covenant, he implies that the first one is old. And anything old and ageing is ready to disappear. (Hebrews 8:6–13 NJB)

This makes [Jesus] the mediator of a new covenant, so that, now that a death has occurred to redeem the sins committed under an earlier covenant, those who have been called to an eternal inheritance may receive the promise. (Hebrews 9:15 NJB)

Every priest stands at his duties every day (in the old covenant) offering over and over again the same sacrifices which are quite incapable of taking away sins. [Jesus], on the other hand, has offered one single sacrifice for sins, and then *taken his seat forever, at the right hand of God*, where he is now waiting *till his enemies are made his footstool*. By virtue of that one single offering, he has achieved the eternal perfection of all who are sanctified. (Hebrews 10:11–14 NJB, words in parentheses added)

When these have been forgiven, there can be no more sin offerings. (Hebrews 10:18 NJB)

This cup is the New Covenant in My blood poured out for you. (Jesus at the Last Supper with His disciples in Luke 22:20 NJB)

Receive the blessing of Father's eternal covenant spoken over you:

May God, who puts all things together,
    makes all things whole,

Who made a lasting mark through the sacrifice of Jesus,
>   the sacrifice of blood that sealed the eternal covenant,

Who led Jesus, our Great Shepherd,
>   up and alive from the dead,

Now put you together, provide you
>   with everything you need to please him,

Make us into what gives him most pleasure,
>   by means of the sacrifice of Jesus, the Messiah.

All glory to Jesus forever and always!
>   Oh, yes, yes, yes. (Hebrews 13:20–21 MSG)

The Duty of Judging

In this era of the new covenant, God handed over the duties of judging to His Son, Jesus.

> The Father judges no one; He has entrusted all judgment to the Son, so that all may honor the Son as they honor the Father. (John 5:22–23 NJB)

Jesus, who came to extend grace and mercy to the world, chose to take upon Himself the verdict of "guilty" so that we who are found in Christ would never be judged by Him.

The only one who has the authority to judge us is, in fact, the One who is 100 percent for us![12]

> In all truth I tell you, whoever listens to My words, and believes in the One Who sent me, has eternal life; without being brought to judgment, such a person has passed from death to life. (John 5:24 NJB)

For God sent His Son into the world not to judge the world, but so that through Him the world might be saved.

No one who believes in Him will be judged, but whoever does not believe is judged already, because that person does not believe in the Name of God's only Son. (John 3:17–18 NJB)

If anyone hears My words and does not keep them faithfully, it is not I Who shall judge such a person, since I have come not to judge the world, but to save the world. Anyone who rejects Me and refuses My words has his judge already: the word itself that I have spoken will be his judge on the last day. (John 12:47–48 NJB)

Because the Father's verdict is final and He has already judged in our favor, the only way we do not receive the Father's judgment of "not guilty" is if we refuse it. In that case, God has not judged us to be separated from Him, but we have judged ourselves, choosing our own judgment on the matter over God's.

A Story of Extreme Grace

Jesus came to perfectly represent His Father in heaven. He did everything He saw the Father doing. Jesus was sent to demonstrate the kingdom exactly the way the Father designed it to be. Therefore, Jesus is perfect theology.

One of the most astounding stories about Jesus in the New Testament tells of when He healed a paralytic man while He was preaching in a house in Capernaum.[13] The word got out that Jesus was in the house, and in a heartbeat the place was packed to the gills. Four men brought a friend who was paralyzed on a stretcher. Their friend needed a God-sized miracle from Jesus, but they had no way to get him through the crowds pressing in around Jesus. So they made a hole in the roof and lowered him right to the King of Glory.

Jesus was thoroughly impressed with their courageous faith. The very first thing He said to the paralyzed man was "Take heart, son: your sins are forgiven."[14]

Maybe, like me, you've read this story many times over without it ever crossing your mind that the paralyzed man never asked for forgiveness. It's impressive enough to talk about the authority Jesus had been given from the Father to openly pronounce such a pardon, but to do so without forgiveness being asked of Him starts to short-circuit our theological formulas. How can God forgive people who have not asked for it?

Remember, Jesus is perfect theology. That means Jesus was doing exactly what He saw the Father doing. Jesus was demonstrating the astounding mystery of the gospel of grace. He displayed the heart of a Father who is so enamored with His children on this earth that He stopped at absolutely nothing to be certain we had a path that would lead straight to His heart … forever!

Romans 5:18 clearly says that Adam's offense in the garden of Eden brought condemnation on *all* humanity. (We were not there to vote on the matter!) Equally, Jesus' perfect sacrifice on the cross set *all* of humanity free and made us right with God. (We weren't around to put our two cents in there, either.) Jesus paid for the forgiveness of the entire world in full.

"Preposterous!" many Christians would cry. "We must choose Christ before we are forgiven." While that has a ring of theological accuracy, what's actually the case is this:

> God pursues each and every one of His children with His love and with a full pardon already secured. Our choice is simply to accept or to decline what has already been completed for us.

Now, before you brand me a heretic, let me assure you that I am fully convinced the only way to the Father is through Jesus, who Himself said, "No one comes to the Father except through Me."[15] There is no other sacrifice than the one by Jesus that makes us perfectly right with our Father. But the truth remains: We are already "in"—unless we decide we don't want the free gift that has been paid for in full.

Love is risky and God risked it all. He put everything on the line, knowing that the object of his affection—His sons and daughters whom He created in His own image to enjoy Him and be enjoyed by Him—would have to choose His pardon and want to be with Him in return.

The only reason you and I have a choice to enter into what has been prepared for us is because it's *already* there for us. God initiates everything first. He reveals and we respond. Forgiveness from God is not something out of our reach that we have to earn. It is something already done that we agree with. If forgiveness were dependent upon you and me and our asking for it, we would all be in deep trouble!

It's time to enter into His rest.

Chapter Reflections

- Where do you need to update your understanding of the new covenant of grace as something you are presently living in rather than a future reality?

- Imagine a courtroom in heaven where you will be sentenced, but you can't be found because Jesus took your place. There isn't a shred of evidence against you. What is your response to such extreme love and grace? Express openly your gratitude to God.

- How has Papa initiated his love, grace, and forgiveness towards you in a way that caused you to respond? What did that response look like?

Chapter 9

It's Time to Rest

❦

You don't have to do a thing to earn My love and approval.
It's already yours.
I simply want you to enjoy Me as I am enjoying you.
The pressure is off.
Relax and agree with how good I am to you.

I told you grace was so amazing you'd think it was almost too good to be true, but it's all God's doing—all His choice—not ours. He didn't ask for our opinion on the matter. Instead, He took the entire matter into His own hands. In the same way He chose to bless Abraham, He says to us:

> It's My choice to bless you and not to curse you. It is My choice to do good to you and display My outrageous favor upon you every day of your life. I will love you extravagantly because I want to. I've purposed this to be the way it is, and I will always make good on My promise.

The religious people of Jesus' day were offended by Him. If what He was saying about the kingdom of God was true, all of their striving to be right with God through their own efforts would amount to a big, fat nothing. Similarly, the religious mind today is offended by the message of radical grace the way it has been given to us by the Father.

Yet the choice remains: Do we want in on this outrageous grace deal? If so, what's our part? Do we even have a part? I believe we do. The one decision we've been given is to believe that Jesus' sacrifice on the cross was completely enough to make us right with God.

> By entering through faith into what God has always wanted to do for us—set us right with him, make us fit for him—we have it all together with God because of our Master Jesus. And that's not all: We throw open our doors to God and discover at the same moment that he has already thrown open his door to us. We find ourselves standing where we always hoped we might stand—out in the wide-open spaces of God's grace and glory, standing tall and shouting our praise. Now that we are set right with God by means of this sacrificial death, the consummate blood sacrifice, there is no longer a question of being at odds with God in any way. (Romans 5:1–2, 9 MSG)

Never at odds with God in any way … doesn't that sound refreshing? Yet some will look at this encouraging passage and still be plagued with the question *Am I believing God enough? Do I have enough faith?*

The problem with such questions is they take the focus off of what Jesus has done and onto self, which is exactly how we get into these self-destructive theological dilemmas. Jesus' answer to the faith question is this: "You have to be like a little child to enter the Kingdom of God."[1]

Instead of looking at this statement of His as another formula you have to get right, stop and reflect on what Jesus is saying. A little baby doesn't question whether she will get milk as she latches onto her mother's breast. That thought wouldn't ever enter her sweet little head. *Of course Mama has milk for me!*

Your heavenly Daddy supplies everything you need and then some because it's His total delight to do so. Faith is never about striving harder or approaching God in just the right manner to get what you need. Faith is trusting, just like a little child who knows *Of course my daddy will take care of me!* If this still sounds like a stretch for you, remember, in the new covenant exchange, everything that belonged to Jesus is now yours—including His faith!

> Let us keep our eyes fixed on Jesus, the author and finisher of our faith. (Hebrews 12:2 NIV)

The key to enjoying all that's yours as a loved and favored child of God is to keep looking at Jesus' sufficiency, not at what you perceive your deficiencies to be.

Constantly focusing on how you think you're doing is a recipe for disaster. Introspection is a killer, because we're brutal on ourselves. Instead, ask the Holy Spirit what He sees. He'll show you areas in your life that are not consistent with your complete new nature in Christ, but He will always do so in a way that encourages you and fills you with hope. And when He does show you an area that requires an upgrade by applying the truth of the cross, He wants you to ask *Him* to do it because He's the only One who can.

Entering In

Abraham is a model of how to receive and enjoy a life of blessing. He entered into what his Father promised him by taking God at His word.

> Abraham entered into what God was doing for him, and that was the turning point. He trusted God to set him right instead of trying to be right on his own. (Romans 4:3 MSG)
>
> When everything was hopeless, Abraham believed anyway, deciding to live not on the basis of what he saw he couldn't

do, but on what God said he would do. (Romans 4:18 MSG)

Now what the law code asked for but we couldn't deliver is accomplished as we, instead of redoubling our own efforts, simply embrace what the Spirit is doing in us. (Romans 8:4 MSG)

Embracing what God does for you is the best thing you can do for him. (Romans 12:1 MSG)

Abraham was able to enter into God's rest by believing in His goodness. The Israelites, however, weren't able to do so. They couldn't leave their wandering in the wilderness to enter the rest of God in the Promised Land because they refused to believe. Today, in the new covenant of grace, we are once again invited to enjoy God's rest—His satisfaction in the completed work of Christ on our behalf.

Everything has been arranged and paid for. The invitations have gone out. All we need to do to enjoy the most amazing life imaginable in Christ is to accept it.

Yes, Father, You are this good! I accept Your invitation of freedom and life bought for me by Jesus. I choose to rest in your outlandish goodness towards me.

Here is the invitation in Scripture:

The conclusion is clear: the original rest is still left in place for God's people. God's rest celebrates His finished work. Whoever enters into God's rest immediately quits his own efforts to add to or complement what God has already perfected. (Hebrews 4:9–10 TMT)

God has wonderful plans for every child of His on this earth. He is an excited Papa who can barely contain Himself because of the surprises He has waiting for us along life's journey. The only way we miss out on all the fun is if we don't believe He's that good.

> So we see they were not allowed to enter and have God's rest, because they did not believe. We who have believed are able to enter and have God's rest. (Hebrews 3:19; 4:3 NCV)

Just like the Israelites in the wilderness, too many believers have been wandering around in circles, waiting for the promises of God that already belong to them. God says to you, "I have set every day as *today* for My promises."[2]

God sees the day when an entire generation will finally agree with how astoundingly good He is. I believe we are that generation!

I also believe we are walking deeper in revival than we understand. Revival is God breathing fresh life into His people—causing Jesus to be our true first love—so that when the harvest of souls comes into the kingdom, they'll be grafted in with a bride who's joyful and passionate for Jesus, not a depressed one who's just getting by.

I've been living in the absolute certainty of my Daddy's extravagant love for me for well over a decade now, and it only gets better. The more I focus on His goodness, the more I see it unfold in my life. I know to the core of my being that Papa is wildly in love with me every second of every day because I'm His precious son. It has absolutely nothing to do with what I do or don't do for Him. Now, that's freedom!

If I were fooling myself into believing a pleasant-sounding lie to make myself feel better, that house of cards would've fallen a long time ago. No, this is the real deal. I'm an extremely happy camper, blessed and highly favored beyond measure. I've entered into the rich and full life the Lord promises to His children, and I'm never going back to an inferior existence.

This invitation into the wonder and awe of our Father's vast, warm love is for every single person on the earth. He invites us into a journey that will take forever to discover, but that's okay, because He's given us all of eternity to find out just how good He really is. This rich and full life is within reach. When Jesus was alive on the earth, He said, "The kingdom of heaven is near!"[3] Now that we are in the new covenant of grace, it gets even better. Now the kingdom of heaven is within![4]

A Confusing Mixture

Most of us don't trust in the saving work of Jesus with the intention of falling back into a works-based self-help program. Initially, the exchange that occurred—our old, miserable, messed-up lives replaced by Christ's perfection in our place—was nothing short of exhilarating. We were suddenly brand new and we could feel it!

But for most, an all-too-common scenario begins to unfold. Ever so slowly, over time, the simplicity of the gospel gets a little more complex. What started out as a celebration of our invigorating freedom somehow turns into a growing list of dos and don'ts that gets increasingly more difficult to navigate and uphold. We begin to judge ourselves mercilessly and beat ourselves up for not behaving in all the right ways. We feel worse and worse about ourselves and we're sure that God feels the same way.

Here's the real kicker. We decide that if we have to live in this misery, we're going to make real sure that everybody else lives in that same misery with us. We begin to judge others, sometimes ruthlessly, believing this to be part of our duty to keep the rest of the world on track. Somewhere along the way, the joy of being set free from the bondage of sin and belonging to our sweet Jesus morphs into the drudgery of a different kind of bondage called striving and performance. After a while, we begin to adopt a mindset that sounds something like this:

God will love me more if… and *God will be pleased with me when…*

How did we get to this place? This isn't what we signed up for. It's certainly not what Jesus died for. It's no wonder so many people have chosen to remove themselves from the religious structure known as the church.

Every child learns early on that if there's no way to win a game, you don't play. The game of relating correctly to God by way of keeping rules perfectly is one you can't win. The only way to win this game is to choose not to play.

Make no mistake: the Church is still alive and well. When God looks upon His Church, He's not gazing on an institution, but on a people who belong to Him.

The true Church is made up of believers who, by their very nature, believe Him.

Those who believe Him know He's a happy Father who loves His children.

Jesus rescued the apostle Paul from a life of extreme religious striving and performance. Once Paul experienced the freedom of resting in his relationship with the Father because of what Christ had done for him, he had zero tolerance for believers who fell back into the performance-based trap of religion. He wrote this pointed message to his friends in Galatia, who'd been duped by religious leaders of the old religious school who were trying to put people back into the chains of legalism—trying to please God by adhering to rules and regulations.

> You crazy Galatians! Did someone put a hex on you? Have you taken leave of your senses? Something crazy has happened, for it's obvious that you no longer have the crucified Jesus in clear focus in your lives. His sacrifice on the cross was certainly set before you clearly enough.
>
> Let me put this question to you: How did your new life begin? Was it by working your heads off to please God? Or was it by responding to God's Message to you? Are you going to continue this craziness? For only crazy people would think they could complete by their own efforts what was begun by God. If you weren't smart enough or strong

enough to begin it, how do you suppose you could perfect it? (Galatians 3:1–3 MSG)

Paul is screaming, "Stop the insanity!" And this from the former rule-keeper of all rule-keepers! Paul knows that saving us and bringing us home safely is all God's doing from start to finish. For some reason, this offends the mind and we find ourselves falling back into the "doing" mode. *Surely it can't be that easy,* we tell ourselves.

This is the same struggle people had in Jesus' day when they approached Him with this anxiety filled question: "What must we do to do the works God requires?" You know what Jesus' simple and straightforward answer was?

"The work of God is this: to believe in the one he has sent."[5] That's it! If there'd been a long list of things we had to do to be approved of by God, don't you think this would have been an opportune time for Jesus to bring it up?

No More Performance

Because we don't fully understand the new covenant of grace, we often wear ourselves out trying to be good and do good things for God, believing this to be the essence of the Christian life.

Jesus, who came to show us the true nature of the Father, spoke these words to a weary world:

> Are you tired? Worn out? Burned out on religion? Come to me. Get away with me and you'll recover your life. I'll show you how to take a real rest. Walk with me and work with me—watch how I do it. Learn the unforced rhythms of grace. I won't lay anything heavy or ill fitting on you. Keep company with me and you'll learn to live freely and lightly. (Matthew 11:28–30 MSG)

I remember the first time I read those words in this refreshing translation. It was as though I was catching Jesus' heart in a way I'd never seen before. I thought, *Could this possibly be true? Could Jesus have really meant that I'm supposed to live freely and lightly? How is that even possible?*

For years, in my zealousness of wanting so badly to be a good son, I had inadvertently traded my status as an acceptable and cherished son for a stage performer who was always one good performance shy of feeling really good about myself. Like everybody, I had what I thought were my good days along with what were clearly my less-than-stellar days. Instead of enjoying each day as a gift—a blank slate from God as His chosen friend—I lived it with the pressure of trying to live up to expectations I thought God had of me. It was exhausting!

My Father, in His graciousness, was saying to me, *Son, you're trying way too hard. Listen to Jesus' words of sanity that speak life, not condemnation.* Looking at the passage again, I peered into the heart of Jesus and heard this:

> If you are burned out on that old system of trying to make yourself better, how about coming to Me and resting instead? Leave behind all of the self-help programs that tell you how to pull yourself up by the bootstraps and dig yourself out of a hole. It doesn't work that way. It never will. Learn about how I choose to live a life of love with My Father and how everything flows from that love relationship. I lived fully reliant on the Holy Spirit, whom I've now sent to live within you. He will teach you how to yield to the life that you were meant to live—a life that is free and light.

This is just the way it is! Our pride gets in the way when we say, *There must be something I have to do. I'll try harder for You, God.*

Do you know what His answer is? *I'm not interested.* In fact, if you persist in trying to earn God's love and acceptance through performance, God will make sure that it doesn't work and that you get good and tired. (It may take years or even decades for you to completely exhaust yourself.) Do you know why? He can't reward your efforts of trying to be good to earn His approval or it would encourage you to keep doing it!

Instead of getting mad about this, give in to the goodness of God on your behalf and let Him have your stubborn insistence to do everything for yourself. This can come from adopting perfectionist tendencies (*If I want something done right, I'll have to do it myself*) or from an independent, orphan spirit (*No one is going to take care of me, so I have to take care of myself*). He'll gladly take either from you in exchange for a spirit of adoption that says, *My Daddy will take care of me now*.

If you are in the habit of making promises to God or to yourself about how you're going to change yourself, I invite you to put those in a mental waste receptacle for the Lord to dispose of properly.

> The best resolution you can make every day of every year for the rest of your life is to choose to believe what God says about who He is and about who you are.

Agree with Him that He is changing you, just as He promised He would.

Trust that He's working everything out for your good, because that's what your heavenly Father lives to do for you. Just like Abraham, you get to enjoy a life of being lavishly blessed by an outrageously good Father simply by agreeing with His huge heart for you.

> While the spirit of the world is obsessed with performance and its due reward, the spirit of God unveils the mystery of his generosity; this cannot be earned, it can only be received as a gift. (1 Corinthians 2:12 TMT)

Paul (who lived most of his life believing that striving to adhere to the strict Law code was the way to please God) wrote this after finding his true freedom in what Christ had accomplished for him:

> If I was "trying to be good," I would be rebuilding the same old barn that I tore down. I would be acting as a charlatan. What actually took place is this: I tried keeping rules and working my head off to please God, and it didn't work. So I quit being a "law man" so that I could be God's

man. Christ's life showed me how, and enabled me to do it. I identified myself completely with him. Indeed, I have been crucified with Christ. My ego is no longer central. It is no longer important that I appear righteous before you or have your good opinion, and I am no longer driven to impress God. Christ lives in me. The life you see me living is not "mine," but it is lived by faith in the Son of God, who loved me and gave himself for me. I am not going to go back on that.

Is it not clear to you that to go back to that old rule-keeping, peer-pleasing religion would be an abandonment of everything personal and free in my relationship with God? I refuse to do that, to repudiate God's grace. If a living relationship with God could come by rule-keeping, then Christ died unnecessarily. (Galatians 2:18–21 MSG)

The problem of trying to please God by living right is very simple—you can't do it! It doesn't work and it never will. Instead, Papa invites you up on His lap and says to you:

My precious child, I've noticed how tired and cranky you've become. You need a nap! My version of a nap is resting from all of your striving. You have My permission to get off the treadmill of performance. It's exhausting and you're not actually getting anywhere. I have a refreshing secret to tell you: there are no hoops to jump through for Me. The pressure is totally off. I cannot let you strive to gain what you already have. I love you and accept you. Look into My eyes and choose to believe Me.

At this point you may need a good cry with the Lord, especially if you have tried with all your might for years and years to please Him, always thinking that you were coming up short. It's okay to have a good cry while Father holds you. As He tenderly does so, He tells you one more thing:

I'm not disappointed with you. I've never been disappointed with you a day in your life. People get disappointed because they have certain expectations of others that are not met. I'm not like that. I already know everything about you and I have no unrealistic expectations of you. I know that you can't save yourself and that you need a Savior. Done! I couldn't possibly be more proud of you than I already am.

Transformation

If you are still feeling like an unlovable child, be encouraged by this story from a good friend of mine, Lorie McNamee, as she shares of her transformation from a performance-based relationship with God into one of intimacy with her heavenly Father:

> I was raised in church. There was never a time when I didn't believe in God. In Sunday school and at home I was taught about right and wrong and that God was watching me. I pictured God as being high up in the skies somewhere looking down on me, watching everything I did, but not in a loving way. I pictured him like Santa, "making a list, checking it twice" to find out if I was "naughty or nice." This idea carried over into adulthood. Like David in the Bible, I knew my transgressions and my sin were always before me. I felt like a failure. I was sure that God the Father disapproved of me and that Jesus' sacrifice was all the more amazing because I was totally unlovable.
>
> When I got married, my husband, Chad, had to continually reinforce his love for me. I always felt unworthy before him. To his credit, he was patient and did not get weary with constantly reminding me that he loved me. He also encouraged me and believed in me. Chad's relationship with God was very different than mine. He had a friendship with God and often spoke of ongoing conversations with Him. I was fascinated and hungry for the same kind of relationship with God.

One day I was driving in the car and I said out loud, "Jesus, is there anything You want to say to me?" Immediately, deep in my spirit, I felt Him say, "I love you. I love you. I love you. I love you. I love you. I love you. I love you. I love you …" It was like waves of the ocean breaking over me. I sobbed. First of all, I didn't really expect to "hear" anything, so it caught me off guard. Second, I didn't expect God to say *that*. My expectation was that if God ever spoke to me, He would point out my faults and tell me I had not measured up to His standard.

Then I went through a very difficult period of my life for four years, struggling with the effects of multiple sclerosis slowly and steadily deteriorating my body. I became increasingly debilitated until I was finally bedridden for a few months. During that time I felt God's loving presence more than ever before. Someone had given us a DVD of a man singing a song he wrote for his daughter about the Father's love for His children. I played that song over and over for five weeks. Every time I played it, Chad would smile at me. I felt like a child sitting in my Father's lap. I felt loved and at peace.

Then I was miraculously and totally healed of MS by Jesus![6] After that I became involved with Blazing Fire Church and began going to their Kingdom Training School of Supernatural Ministry. Every week I heard about their core values, and always the emphasis was on the Father's love. I remember one teacher, Donna Fuller, sharing about a childhood upbringing similar to mine and how she had come to know the Father in a different way. I remember her husband, Art, sharing that he had to sit under the teaching of God's love for a few years before it finally sank in. I remember Brent saying that God couldn't be disappointed in us because in order to be disappointed, God would have to have had expectations for us that were not fulfilled, and that was impossible because God already knew everything about us.

I replayed the class tapes, read Brent's weekly encouragement e-mails encouraging me that my heavenly Daddy loved me. I pored over the Bible in a new way. I began to see things in a different light. I meditated on the Psalms and how David reveled, even wallowed, in the Father's love.

Then one day, I realized I was different. There was not a dramatic event that I could point to, but gradually my mindset had changed. I no longer felt unloved and unlovable. I had come to a place where I no longer doubted God's love at all. With it came freedom and a new love for others. Now when I pray for people, I don't pray out of desperation, but out of confidence in the Father's love for them. I had to grasp God's love for me before I could let His love flow through me.

I can truly say with Psalm 34:4–5, "I sought the Lord, and He answered me; He delivered me from all my fears. Those who look to Him are radiant; their faces are never covered with shame."

Lorie's story is typical in that there was a process she engaged in of choosing to believe the truth even before it felt completely real to her. Then, at some point, she realized she was different and saw things in an entirely new light. Jesus likened the kingdom of God to a seed becoming a tree, or a bit of yeast making its way throughout a batch of dough (Luke 13:18–21). In other words, the change is continual but you can't really point to the exact times and places the transformation occurred. One day, you look at your life and say, "Huh! I wonder when I became such a big tree." Your Father says that He will finish what He has started in you—and He means it!

No More Beating Yourself Up

You have a decision to make. If being really hard on yourself isn't producing in you the life you had hoped for, you must make a choice to proceed a different way. Make a choice to rest.

Believing the truth and choosing to stay in this place of rest can be challenging when conflicting thoughts come streaming through our minds. When that happens, we often want to beat ourselves up for having such shocking thoughts. God is not shocked at all and He can handle it.

The problem with beating yourself up is you're actually bolstering the enemy's lies. One of satan's main tasks is to accuse believers.[7] When we say or even think horrible things about ourselves—ugly self-talk—we are actually agreeing with the enemy, who is a deceiver and a liar. Why would we ever align ourselves with that kind of negativity, when its purpose is to tear us down and take us out of the picture? Beating yourself up isn't helping you one bit or drawing you closer to God, who has never left you.

The battlefield of the enemy to rob your joy takes place in your mind. It's the only battleground he has because your spirit already knows the truth of who you are. Since the enemy has been defeated by Christ at the cross,[8] his only hope for attacking your mind is to use deception. In other words, if he can get you to believe the lie, it appears real to you, even though it isn't. Therefore, it's important that we not give any credence or weight to false ideas.

> For although we are human, it is not by human methods that we do battle. The weapons with which we do battle are not those of human nature, but they have the power, in God's cause, to demolish fortresses. It is ideas that we demolish, every presumptuous notion that is set up against the knowledge of God, and we bring every thought into captivity and obedience to Christ. (2 Corinthians 10:3–5 NJB)

The next time you hear words in your head that don't match up with what your Father says is true about you, ask Him to shine His light on those thoughts and to share with you what He thinks about you instead. I encourage you to journal His thoughts toward you.

As you sit with Papa God, ask Him out loud, "What do You think about me?"

Then linger and listen for a moment or two. Begin writing the up-lifting words you sense from within. As you learn to value His ever-streaming thoughts of love and affection for you, His opinion will trump the negative self-talk that doesn't reflect who you really are.

If you're still learning what His voice is like, allow me to give you an example. The lies in your head might sound something like this: *I'm a loser. I'm so stupid. I'll never amount to anything.* Papa's voice of truth sounds something like this:

> Son/Daughter, you're not a loser—you're a lover and a winner forever. You're never stupid. Even if you forget who you are at times, I will keep reminding you that you are royalty and you are perfect for Me. I've given you My heart to feel as I feel and My mind to think as I think. And the part about not amounting to anything? What a laugh! Of all the beautiful things I've made in creation, you are the most beautiful. I've put My own resurrection spirit within you to assure you of victory and success!

Jesus said we will know the truth and the truth will set us free.[9] The Holy Spirit has been given to us as a gift—a counselor and friend who will constantly remind us of the truth that transforms us.[10] I encourage you to ask for His help often. He loves to assist you!

> Holy Spirit, I invite You to transform me. Change the way I think. Change the way I look at life. Help me to see my

Papa the way He really is. Help me to see myself the way my Father does so I can look in the mirror, see what He sees in me, and say, "Wow!" Father, I believe Your love for me is real and unchanging, and I receive Your love. I want to be a lover of people the way You are. I give You my full permission to use me to lavishly pour on others what You so lavishly pour into me.

The Holy Spirit will teach you how to continually agree that you are right with God all the time, not just when you feel like you are. You are secure in Him. Believing that like a little child is your rest. You could sit in a chair and do absolutely nothing today and God would be pleased with you beyond measure—thrilled to call you His son or daughter.

Does He have things for you to do? Sure. But until you know His deep pleasure for you apart from anything you do or don't do, you will still be striving to earn His acceptance. Only by resting in the completion of all that Christ purchased for you, especially that you are perfectly right with your Father, will your life begin to blossom effortlessly and impact others with His love in ways that are transformational for them.

Righteousness by faith realised means unlimited friendship with God. (Romans 5:1 TMT)

God's Not Comparing You to Anybody Else

One important component of resting is resisting the temptation to compare yourself with others. All that will accomplish is to cause you to feel "less than." You aren't meant to be like anyone else, so why would others become your standard?

> God has no desire for you to be a copy of
> someone else. You are an original masterpiece
> that He gazes on with great admiration.

Several years ago, I was freed up from needless comparisons by this truth from Steve Shultz. Here is a portion of an encouraging word he gave titled, "God Grades on the Cross, Not on the Curve":

> Never been graded on the curve? Instead of an "A" being given to those who received 90% or more correct answers, the teacher changed the rules. He (or she) graded "on the curve" which meant they would grade from the top STUDENT in the class, rather than from total-points-possible.
>
> God's standard is not the top-performing disciple. I'm relieved that God doesn't score us that way. Look, we already too easily compare ourselves with others. The last thing we need (or could take) is the LORD grading us by comparing us to "the best student—the best disciple" or the second best disciple, or ANY disciple for that matter.
>
> Actually, God grades only on perfection—the perfection of THE CROSS. In Christ, we are all graded on THE CROSS! Jesus got an "A+" with about 100 trillion extra credit points—enough to secure an A+ for every man, woman and child, past, present, and future who chooses to graduate and join Jesus. The CROSS paid for it all— all our sins, all our shortcomings, all our mistakes, all our attitudes, all our judgments.
>
> It doesn't depend on whether I've had a bad-hair day or a bad-Christian day. The CROSS paid for it all. The reason this is good to know is this; As soon as I work on and fix every relationship in my life, confess every known sin in my life, and make sure I'm walking in Holiness—as surely

as I've done all those things, I'll need to confess and fix a whole new string of things tomorrow.

God gives you a PERFECT GRADE because of the Cross (since you received Christ and His death). So why are you so concerned, having received a perfect grade. If you received an A+ in Heaven based on the CROSS ALONE such that Resurrection Life now flows through you—HOW MUCH MORE then—will your life be taken care of, filled, provided for, encouraged, restored, and forever saved THROUGH HIS LIFE!

Thank You, Jesus, that You did it ALL![11]

Don't Worry about Anything

Don't worry about anything, but in everything, by prayer and petition, with thanksgiving, present your requests to God, and the peace of God, which transcends all understanding will guard your hearts and minds in Christ Jesus. (Philippians 4:6–7 NIV)

With the barrage of negative news coming at you from every direction, you have a moment-by-moment choice before you. The choice is this: "Whose report am I going to believe?"

God's report is this: "You have been chosen by Me to be My blessed and highly favored child and to be a light in the midst of darkness. All things are working for your good at all times." But the world's report, fueled by fear and the enemy's intimidation, is highly discouraging by its very nature.

The world says, "Fret! Be anxious!"

God says to you, "Peace. Be still."

The world says, "Lose sleep worrying! All is lost!"

God says to you, "I am for you. I am in total control. All is going according to My plan."

He assures you of a peace that surpasses all understanding. That means you'll have to give up your demand to have everything all figured out in your mind. That's still you trying to take care of you. God's peace, which bypasses your reasoning, comes as a direct feed from His Spirit to your spirit. So even when your mind can't come up with the solutions, your spirit is already at rest. Next you listen to the truth of the Spirit of Christ within you and let Him restore the peace of your emotions and your thinking back into their proper alignment.

Take a deep breath (go ahead, do it right now) and remind yourself, *All is well. I have a Good Shepherd who promised to take exceptional care of me. I am my Beloved's and He is mine. All things are working out for my good. Ahhhhhhhhhh … I will worry about nothing!*

Jesus says to you:

> Peace I leave with you. My peace I give to you. I do not give to you as the world gives. Do not let your hearts be troubled and do not be afraid!" (John 14:27 NIV)

There is a river from God's heart to yours that never stops flowing. It refreshes and rejuvenates you with all the righteousness, peace, and joy of his magnificent kingdom.[12] Why don't you stop right now for a moment and enjoy the constant current of this heavenly river that flows right through you? Some of you will actually feel it and others will be encouraged just to know it's there.

Soaring Higher

> Though youths grow weary and tired, and vigorous young men stumble badly, yet those who wait for the Lord will gain new strength; they will sprout wings like eagles, they will run and not get tired, they will walk and not become weary. (Isaiah 40:30–31 NASB)

That word *wait* actually means to be entwined or braided with the Lord. Waiting isn't an inactive "twiddling your thumbs and doing nothing until God shows up." He's already here! As our hearts are entwined with His, we gain new strength, because when we are in tune with His affections, we know all is well and we will be taken care of.

As our spirit and His are braided together, the wind from His Spirit lifts us up effortlessly so we soar upward like an eagle.

We ride the updrafts above the low-lying clouds of depression, discouragement, and anxiety, where the sky is always clear and the sun is always shining.

Recently, while spending time sitting with the Lord and choosing to release all my cares to Him that He already had the solutions for, I experienced an exhilarating vision. I could see vivid pictures in my mind of an ongoing adventure. This is what I saw and encountered:

> I am rising up with the wings of an eagle, being lifted effortlessly higher by the wind of Your Spirit beneath my wings. The air is crisp and clear. There are no worries up here—no predators. I sense the direction of the wind. I adjust my wings ever so slightly to use the power of the wind to lift me higher still.
>
> I sail around a mountain and there I spot a Shepherd—up high on the mountain, tending to some sheep. He looks right at me, smiles, and gives me the thumbs-up with one hand, while the other is still holding on to His staff. As I continue to soar with the wind, His smile becomes a full-throated laugh. He approves, and He is enjoying me enjoying my freedom.
>
> I continue on and soon I fly over a crystal-blue sea. There are no limits to where and how far I can go. I am not tired in the least bit—no drudgery, no exhaustion, just exhilaration and peace as the sun-drenched peaks of water swiftly pass below me.
>
> The Lord asks me, "Where do you want to go next?"
>
> My immediate response is "I want to go to You. I can travel anywhere, but my destination is You!"

Suddenly, I am flying right toward my Savior, with leather fastened around His outstretched arm, awaiting my descent. I effortlessly swoop down to Him, landing on His arm with my talons grasping the leather. Jesus is on an island, but not one surrounded by water. Instead, it is high up in the air, with a yellowish-whitish glow all about and with His castle in the distance behind Him. Jesus strokes my head and tells me, "You're doing *so* well! Wasn't that fun? You can come and land here with Me anytime you want when you need My assurance. But I'm not only here holding you and stroking your head. I'm the Shepherd you passed on the mountainside, and I'm in you wherever you go."

I choose to stay perched on Jesus for the time being. He's happy with my choice. He says, "Okay, then, let Me show you something." He turns around and walks with me, still on His arm, toward His castle.

As we draw closer, I see attendants all around His castle—animals, angels, and saints who have gone on before us—intermingled and all exuberantly joyful. All of them are now focusing their full attention on Jesus' approach. Somehow, Jesus' gaze affirms and engages with each and every one, which causes their faces to beam brighter still, knowing they are important to Him—honored and celebrated by Him.

We walk around the outside of His mansion (He lets me know we can go look in there another time), and He takes me to a garden in the back. There He shows me a small tree. Somehow I am instantly aware that I am that tree as well as the eagle on His arm. He lets me know how meticulously and tenderly He cares for that tree. He shows me the fine detail on each leaf as it passes between His thumb and forefinger. He shows me fruits of many kinds that are growing on this tree and has me smell the exotic fragrance of each.

He says, "I *love* this tree! It's My favorite one in the garden." I know it's true and He means it. Then He steps back and sweeps His arm in a wide arc around Him, saying, "And these are My other favorites." As far as my eyes can see are billions of trees. Each one is cared for with equal affection and intentionality. Not one is overlooked. Not one is even partly diseased or dying, because Jesus only sees what the Father has lovingly fashioned.

Jesus looks back at me and says,

"Never doubt My love for you.
My grounds will be filled with fully mature
trees bearing all kinds of amazing fruit,
and I will grow each tree personally with My love.
Not one will be lost. Not one will fail to grow."

I look straight into His eyes and I know He means it.

Then Jesus says, "Now I will show you exactly what I see." Instantly, every single tree is monstrous in size, perfect in dimension, and stunning in color and fragrance—each one different, yet painting a landscape together that is breathtaking!

Jesus laughs heartily and says, "These are My oaks of righteousness! Each one is displaying My glory. Aren't they beautiful? They're perfect and they're Mine."

That was the end of that visionary experience with the Lord, but I knew that I could go back there with Him anytime I chose to do so. As usually happens, the Lord began to remind me of where His Word backed up the experience He gave me. One such Scripture that immediately came to mind was this:

He will give them a crown of beauty
  in place of mourning,

A mantle of praise
  in place of discouragement.

They will be called Oaks of Righteousness,
  Planted by the Lord to glorify Himself. (Isaiah 61:3
CEB)

The more we choose to entwine our hearts with the Lord, the more we will have experiential encounters of His goodness. We have to be careful not to want somebody else's experiences when we hear about them. I share my encounters with you to increase the expectation in your heart for something wonderful to happen in your relationship with your heavenly Father, but He will interact differently with every single child of His. The way He interacts with you has everything in the world to do with how He wired your personality and your interests.

Although you can't *make* experiences happen with God, the more time you spend aware of His presence and talking with Him—getting away from the clatter of the world's noise—the more real your encounters with Him will be.

> It is written: "What man's eyes have never perceived, nor man's ears heard any rumors of; there existed not even a hint of evidence of any importance for man to speculate about in his imagination; concerning the magnitude of what God has put in place for the redemption of the human race, he unveiled to those who intertwine with his thoughts." (1 Corinthians 2:9 TMT)

Realizing you are entwined with God and believing His heart for you will keep your thoughts centered more on Him and less on yourself and how you think you're doing. On this journey we're on with God, we can get down on ourselves if we don't think we're where we ought to be. The truth is that all of us are still in the catch-up phase of apprehending and living in all that took place when we received our brand-new life in Christ.

To the degree that you believe who you already are in Christ, you will walk in what you already have!

In light of that, I hear God saying to each one of you:

Chillax and enjoy Me in the journey more! Enjoy yourself more too. It's good to laugh, My child. I know your life doesn't always look the way you think it should, but I assure you that I am taking you to good places. And don't be so hard on yourself as we travel together. I am constantly changing and molding you to look just like My Son, Jesus, and I know just how to do it in your life. I have given you a heart of flesh,[13] one that is responsive and sensitive to My touch and My voice. Yes, you *do* hear My voice[14] and I am lovingly teaching you that responding to My Spirit within you is your lifeline. I want to remind you that anything the enemy does to try to slow you down, I will use to accelerate your growth. I am trustworthy. I am faithful. I am good in all that I do. I am convincing you that the death blow of My Son's death on the cross to your old sin nature was 100 percent complete. Nothing from your old way of life has power over you any longer.[15] You live solely to please Me now. You are Mine. I won't share you with another. I am causing a distaste in you for anything that draws you away from Me. I have put within you a voracious appetite for My presence. You will continually eat from My tree of life and continually drink from My river of living water. I have plans to make this next year for you one of massive victory. You will stand at the end of this year, look back, and be amazed at all I have done. Be strong and courageous![16]

Because your Father really likes it when you agree with Him, speak these truths out loud as many times as it takes to believe His heart for you.

> My amazing Father, I believe You are good *all* the time! All You can be to me is good. I accept Your invitation to walk in the unforced rhythms of grace and to live freely and lightly with You. I choose to lay down my striving and take a real rest in You. I don't have to do anything to earn my way into Your affections and love for me. I'm Yours! I'm Your wanted child. You love me. You adore me You'll never leave me. I'll enjoy You all the days of my life. I will enjoy more and more intimacy with You as we take longer and longer walks together. I say yes to all of Your advances toward me. Take me into the depths of Your heart where I will get lost in Your love and never find the way out!

Chapter Reflections

- If you truly believed you were never at odds with God in any way, how would that change how you relate to Him, especially the times when you feel like you've blown it?

- Where do you need to enter into the rest by taking God at His word in your life?

- Are you living in the simplicity of the gospel of grace or are you trying to relate correctly with God by trying your hardest to keep the rules? If it's the latter, are you tired and ready to not play that game anymore? Ask the Lord to take all the pressure off!

- Write in a journal God's thoughts toward you. Get still and ask Him, "Papa, what do you think about me?" Write down the impressions you receive.

- How does it feel to not have to compare yourself to anyone else and to know that God sees you as perfect because of Christ?
- In what situations do you need to believe God's report and give up your demand to have everything all figured out in your mind?
- How would your life look if you always lived in the "unforced rhythms of grace"?

SECTION THREE

ॐ

Living a Life of Love that Matters

Transforming Your World

Chapter 10

Know Your Greatness
and Walk in It

❦

My child, you are great beyond measure!
The more I reveal Myself to you, the more you are like Me,
because what you behold you become, from glory to glory!
You were meant to be a world changer,
loving one heart at a time and
releasing My kingdom wherever you go.

Once upon a time there was an exceptionally good and kind King who had a Son whom He loved very much. The King had a place in His heart for all the children in His kingdom, so He adopted them all. (Kings can do whatever they want!) The problem was that most of the children had been incorrectly taught that the King was an angry man who frowned at kids and who punished them severely anytime they made a mistake. So the King thought up new and fun ways every single day to show His great love for all of His children.

He always had time for each child, making every single one feel extra special in a hundred different ways. Every day more and more children believed who the King really was—someone who loved, cherished, and enjoyed every favored child of His. At nighttime, He would hold all of His children close to Himself and open an amazing book of mysteries and dreams, and He would read to them. The children would fall asleep with wonderful visions in their heads of the greatness the King spoke about each of them from this book. The children who received the King's love were wildly happy children.

One night the King brought His children close and said, "I need you to take this love and kindness I've shown you to the other children in My Kingdom who still think I'm mean and unhappy. Would you love them and tell them of the good times we've had together? Would you let them know that they're invited to have fun with Me too? And would you also tell them about My special book of mysteries and dreams that have their names written in it? I will send you with My ring so you'll have My full authority to secure everything you need as you reach out to these ones I dearly love. You can come back as often as you want to get more of My hugs and kisses and affirmation, and if you ever forget the dreams and mysteries I told you about, ask Me and I'll tell you again. You make Me very happy! And as you go out to my adopted ones who don't yet know how much I love them, you are fulfilling My dream that all will know Me as I really am."

> A field that drinks up the rain that has fallen frequently on it, and yields the crops that are wanted by the owners who grew them, receives God's blessing. (Hebrews 6:7 NJB)

We Represent the King's True Heart

We're massively blessed children of the King! We're a green, lush field, drinking up the rain—soaking in the passion of the Lord like sponges taking in God's affirmation and lapping up His love. And God has designed us to go out with His love and give it away. We are the expression of the Father's love to those who don't yet believe how good He is. When we step out to love people and walk in the power of God's kingdom with the purpose of drawing them into the Father's affection, we are yielding the crops that we have been destined to yield.

> As a representative of your Father's heart, your job description is to find any excuse to encourage and bless everyone you come in contact with.

Never choosing to curse, cut down, or berate another of God's treasures, you will build people up with words of affirmation and share a kind smile for those who walk past you on the streets. You will release the love that has so lavishly been given to you by your heavenly Daddy. Freely you have received, so freely you will give it away. You will send the passion of God's love around the world by transforming one heart at a time. You were born in this exact time in history to impact it positively for God's purposes. You are a world changer! The more you enjoy Him, the more your life will impact scores of people, sometimes without your even trying, because you will leak His love everywhere you go!

Just How Special Are You?

God's glory—His very nature—is displayed throughout creation.

The heavens declare the glory of God. (Psalm 19:1 NKJV)

First Corinthians 15:41 reminds us:

The sun has its own glory, the moon another glory and the stars yet another glory; and the stars differ among themselves in glory. (NJB)

When you look up at one of the 600,000,000,000,000,000,000,000 stars (the latest scientific estimate, though scientists acknowledge more stars are continually being born), you realize that particular star is different from every other one. Each star carries a unique glory that displays an aspect of God that no other star carries in the same way. It's head-spinning, to say the least. And those are just the stars! Every plant, every flower, every animal, every sea creature, and even every insect, from the top of Mount Everest to the depths of the sea, fathoms below the surface of the water, all display unique aspects of our Creator God.

He is so vast, so magnificent, so much more brilliantly creative than anything we could begin to wrap our minds around, it takes all of creation together to begin to paint a picture, albeit an incomplete one, of how jaw-dropping amazing He really is!

Take a moment to reflect upon the most beautiful place you've ever enjoyed in nature. I've stood at the top of Yosemite Falls, transfixed by the breathtaking sight of massive volumes of water dramatically cascading a few thousand feet below. I've gazed with tremendous appreciation and wonder at deep purple-and-orange sunsets off the shores of Maui. I've marveled at the overwhelming majesty of huge California redwood trees towering above me, reaching into the sky. I've sat for hours at a time on the shores of Lake Tahoe, mesmerized by its panoramic beauty.

Do you have in mind that special image that takes your breath away with its beauty?

Are you ready for this? When God crafted that most beautiful place, He called it *good*.[1] It was not until He created His crowning glory, man and woman in His own image—including you and me—that He called His creation *very good!*[2] The same Father who put His unique glory into each of the elements of His creation saved the best for last. He's the One who says of you,

"When I created you, I truly outdid Myself. You're the very best part of My creation. You're My absolute favorite!"

On his 1994 album *Poiema*, Michael Card wrote:

> The Bible tells us that we are God's masterpieces (*poiema* in Greek); not only creatures, but His creations, His poems (Ephesians 2:10). We are living epistles (2 Corinthians 3:3). And so, our lives are meant to be listened to, because it is God who is speaking into and out of and through the symphony of the years, and the masterpiece of a lifetime.

The beauty and majesty of how He fashioned you far surpasses the grandeur of everything else He created.

> What is it about man that God cannot get him out of His thoughts? Why would God bother to benefit the son of man? Why would God make so much of man? He has made man all but equal to Himself, He crowned him with His own glory and dignity and appointed him in a position of authority over all the works of His hands. (Hebrews 2:6–7 TMT)

God not only loves you with a passion that surpasses anything you thought you knew about passion, but He says to you, "Let's rule My kingdom together!" Of course, that means it has to be done according to His specs—with love, grace, honor, and mercy, but also with power, signs, and wonders. We're supposed to see the impossible invade this earth. This is why Jesus, when asked by His followers how to pray, responded:

> This, then, is how you should pray: "Our Father in heaven, hallowed be your name, your kingdom come, your will be done, on earth as it is in heaven." (Matthew 6:9–10 NIV)

Jesus was instructing us to know who our Father is and to realize we have His permission to usher the reality of His kingdom into this world. You are crowned with God's own glory and dignity, and you've been given a position of authority in His kingdom. It looks like you and God have some work to do together!

People on this earth will come to know God through those of us who know Him as He really is. Once we know the greatness of who we are as carriers of God's glory, there's nothing to stop us from representing Him accurately across the earth with love and power.

Heaven's Breaking In

One such love-and-power encounter happened for me many years ago when I began to experience the gift of healing that was part of my inheritance in Christ. An employee I was working with, Sandy,[3] had broken her back falling out of a second-story window when she was a teenager. Her back had never healed properly, and now, in her forties, she often had severe pain to deal with. This particular day, Sandy had reinjured her back and was sitting in excruciating pain with a hard back brace around her torso while attempting to work at her desk. I told her about several amazing healing miracles I had seen recently and asked if she wanted me to pray for her to be healed. She readily agreed. But before I prayed I talked with her and found out that while Sandy had grown up in a Christian home, she had a hard time believing God really loved her because of a religious-performance message she'd picked up along the way. She didn't feel she measured up to God's standards and, therefore, wasn't worthy to receive His love.

I had the privilege of sharing about God's affection and approval for her as His daughter. Then I began to declare His healing power to her severely injured back. I commanded bones to move back into place, and within seconds both of us heard popping noises as Sandy's back was quickly realigning! Because this kind of instantaneous miracle was pretty new to me at the time, and because she was starting to cry, I was initially afraid that something worse was happening and she would be in even more pain. But when I asked Sandy why she was crying, through tears of gratitude she excitedly said, "There's no pain! I've lived the last thirty years in pain and it's completely gone!"

Then she added something that made *me* start to cry. She said, "I can't believe God would love me this much to do this for me. My Father loves me!" With that, she took off her brace and danced around the room with childlike giddiness, celebrating her healing and the assurance of the love of her heavenly Father, who adored her as His precious princess.

I saw Sandy occasionally over the next five years or so, and during that time pain never once returned to her perfectly healed back. She also continued to grow in the depth of her relationship with her heavenly Father, whom she knew loved her with all His heart.

Great Beyond Measure

In the past several decades a resurgence of superhero movies has hit the big screen. Through the years have come Superman, Wonder Woman, Batman, Spider-Man, The Fantastic Four, X-Men, The Incredible Hulk, Iron Man, Thor, Captain America, and a host of others. For some of you, even mentioning the names of some of these Defenders of Justice is causing your blood to pump a little faster, vividly retrieving from your store of memories heroic exploits that saved our world from certain destruction.

There's a reason for the widespread, compelling draw of these super-human characters. Something deep inside of people, who feel their lives are frittering away without meaning, is crying out to make a genuine difference in this world. Sure, we may not be able to spin the globe back on its axis to reverse time as Superman did, but we all want in some real way to change the world for the better, because that's what we were made to do.

> We instinctively know we were born for supernatural, extraordinary living—born to be world changers.

We were created by our Father to know Him and to do great exploits![4]

Did you know that even creation itself is groaning and waiting for us to walk in the greatness of who we are and what we carry?

> For the creation waits in eager expectation for the children of God to be revealed. (Romans 8:19 NIV)

Being made in the image of our Creator, we're great beyond measure. At the moment of our spiritual birth, we were infused with the same resurrection power that raised Jesus Christ from the dead![5] Somehow, all of God's created order will experience a release into freedom as we fully step into our freedom of knowing and walking in who we truly are.

Jesus knew who He was. He was God's beloved and massively favored Son, the perfect ambassador of His Father's kingdom, and the inheritor of absolutely everything that belonged to His Dad.

The question is: Do *you* know who *you* are?

> It was fitting that God, for whom and through whom everything exists, should, in bringing many sons to glory, make perfect through suffering the leader of their salvation. For the consecrator and the consecrated are all of the same stock; that is why he is not ashamed to call them brothers. (Hebrews 2:10–11 NJB)

Jesus' status as God's beloved Son is exactly the same status you have as God's son or daughter. Exactly the same! That phrase "all of the same stock" is also translated "we form a single whole" with Jesus. Do you realize the ramifications of that? There's no separating us from Him. He shares His identity with us, and we are perfectly one with Him.

The Mirror Translation puts that same verse like this:

> Because both He who performed the rescuing act and those rescued and restored to innocence, originate from the same source, He proudly introduces them to be identified as His immediate family.

How much better can this get? Jesus has His arm around you, beaming, so very proud, and says about you, "This is my awesome bro! This is my amazing sis! We carry the same spiritual genes and Dad loves us all the same."

Jesus, who was given all authority in heaven and on earth by our Father, says to us:

> You're a purebred from heaven, just like Me. You're made of what I'm made of. And what's Mine is yours. Let's all use the authority Dad's given us. Go and rock the world with His love, grace, and power. I showed you how, and

now I'll go with you to the ends of the earth, because I'm your true Brother and I've got your back. We're family!

Kris Vallotton wrote this about our greatness in his book *The Supernatural Ways of Royalty*:

> For with His blood the Holy One of Radiance purchased rotten, ragged sinners and recreated us into His righteous, reigning Saints!
>
> We are not just soldiers of the cross; we are heirs to the throne. The divine nature permeates our souls, transforms our minds, transplants our hearts, and transfigures our spirits. We were made to be vessels of His glory and vehicles of His light.
>
> Perhaps we are better exemplified as the beautiful daughter who will ascend the throne through marriage, for she is betrothed to the Prince of Peace. The Bridal Chamber is being built, the feast is being prepared, and the Bride is making herself ready. Alternatively, we may be called the Children of God, the Engaged Bride, a Royal Priesthood, the Apple of His Eye, and a New Creation, but above all, one thing is for certain: We have captivated the heart of our Lover. Burning with desire, He has mounted His white horse, assembled a majestic entourage, and is making His way toward the planet!
>
> Meanwhile back on earth, God's people are rising and beginning to shine in this present darkness. His Royal Army is spreading the King's glory all over the earth as we take dominion of this planet back from the defeated one. Equipped with the light of the Father, His sons are finding buried treasure in the hearts of men that was once covered by rocks of offense, thorns of treachery, and relics of religion. Armed with the power of the Holy Spirit and commissioned to re-present the King's Son, we are healing the sick, raising the dead, and displacing devils. Paupers

are becoming princes and princesses as a result, and the kingdom of this world is becoming the Kingdom of our God![6]

Sons and daughters of the Most High King, you are warriors bred for victory! Your zealous Lover is gazing upon you, not wanting anything to hinder you from the depth of intimacy you were designed to enjoy with Him. The strong justice of Father God is rising up in this hour.[7]

His justice is not coming *against* you who are in Christ— you who have been paid for in full by the blood of Jesus on the cross. His justice is *for* you and coming *against* the forces of evil that have been tearing at His bride.

To you, the Lord says:

> Who is like you, O victorious people? Yahweh is the shield that protects you and the sword that leads you to triumph. Your enemies will try to corrupt you, but you yourself will trample on their backs! (Deuteronomy 33:29 NJB)

This will happen, not because we are strong in ourselves, but because God has determined it to be so. God is our protector. He is our sharp sword that assures us of victory. And since we are perfectly made in His image, it shouldn't come as a surprise that He says to us:

> [I] have made you like a warrior's sword. (Zechariah 9:13 NJB)

In other words, Christ in us is continually piercing the darkness with slashes of glory fire! Yet there's even more to His justice on our behalf. He implores us:

> Come back to the fortress, you prisoners waiting in hope. This very day, I vow, I shall make it up to you twice over. (Zechariah 9:12 NJB)

As only God can do, He's determined not only to make up for the enemy's attempts to corrupt us, but to give us back double anything stolen from us as we choose to rest in His goodness. Papa says to you, "Arise, My victorious warrior! Arise in the power of My strength and keep going."

First John 5:4 (NJB) says, "Every child of God overcomes the world. And this is the victory that has overcome the world—our faith." Our assured victory comes by faith, our agreement as a little child that God is good all the time and He will do exactly what He's promised to do. He's made us overcomers!

> Because the Lamb is *Lord of lords* and *King of kings*, he will defeat them, he and his followers, the called, the chosen, the trustworthy. (Revelation 17:14 NJB)

Partnering with God to Change History

So what do we do with all this greatness? Isn't that the real question? Our job description is very clear, actually. It's spelled out for us in 2 Corinthians 5:18–20 (NLT):

> And all of this is a gift from God, who brought us back to himself through Christ. And God has given us this task of reconciling people to him. For God was in Christ, reconciling the world to himself, no longer counting people's sins against them. And he gave us this wonderful message of reconciliation. So we are Christ's ambassadors; God is making his appeal through us. We speak for Christ when we plead, "Come back to God!"

Our clear task is to represent God accurately to this world, letting people know God is for them, not against them. We were made right with God, not because of anything we did, but only because of what Christ did on our behalf.

We are Christ's ambassadors. Authority is given to an ambassador to represent his or her own country in another region of the world.

Within the embassy, that ambassador enjoys all the rights and privileges of his or her country of origin.

Similarly, Christ has given us His full authority to represent Him and His kingdom of grace and love on this earth. While doing so, we have all the rights and privileges of our true country of origin—heaven.

We get to accurately portray the heart of Jesus, whose stated life mission was this:

> The Spirit of the Lord is on me, because he has anointed me to proclaim good news to the poor. He has sent me to proclaim freedom for the prisoners and recovery of sight for the blind, to set the oppressed free, to proclaim the year of the Lord's favor. (Luke 4:18–19 NIV)

Like Jesus, our message to the world must be "Your heavenly Father loves you as His very own. He has done everything to make His children right with Him. You are included. You are invited. All expenses have been paid. Do you want in?"

Is that really God's heart for people before they've repented? Absolutely! That's the good news. Otherwise, how would anyone be saved? We love God only because He first loved us.[8] It's the kindness of God that leads us to repentance.[9] As people see His kindness and mercy, they turn away from a path that was causing destruction onto a path of life and love. It's right to tell others of God's true heart for them before they are saved. As soon as they see and know the real Father and the real Savior, they will choose to jump in with both feet. By sharing the good news as it really is, who wouldn't want in?

You get to accept others and value them simply because they're sons or daughters of your Father, made in His glorious image.

> You are the bringer of very good news: that the love
> they've always longed for, they already have.

And you have the awesome privilege of loving people and watching them bloom into whoever God created them to be, as His ambassadors who carry His presence to the world.

Show Me Your Glory

How can God be so certain we will represent Him well? "Doesn't He know what we're made of?" you might ask. Yes, He does. But more important, God knows what *He's* made of, and He's deposited a measure of His own glorious character inside each one of us. Our supremely confident Father left nothing to chance. He already assured our triumphant outcome by placing within us His own Spirit, making us carriers of His glory.

What does it mean for us to be carriers of God's glory? To answer that we need to look back at Moses' request in Exodus 33:18, where he pleads, "Lord, show me your glory!"

God was willing to do so, but He set the terms of what that would look like. He says to his friend Moses, "All right, then, I will allow My goodness to pass by in front of you, displaying My true character so you can know how good I really am."[10]

Oftentimes, believers today read this story with envy, thinking, *If only I could see God the way Moses got to,* not realizing that we have it way better than Moses ever did.

Moses came back down the mountain from meeting with God and people saw the glory of God on Moses' face. Just by being around the extreme kindness, goodness, and mercy of God, Moses' face beamed. But soon after, that glorious countenance started to fade, so Moses put a veil over his face because he didn't want the Israelite people to see the glory dissipate.[11]

Why would the glory of God fade from Moses? Because it was external! That's the nature of the difference between the old covenant and the new. In the old covenant, when Moses asked to see God's glory, God said, "I'll let My goodness pass *in front of* you." In the new covenant of grace (God making His home inside of us), when we ask God, "Show me Your glory," His answer is:

"Look in the mirror!"

God's goodness lives in you. God's joy resides in you. God's peace dwells in you. God's loving-kindness is embodied in you. That very same goodness that passed before Moses has made His home in you.

If you are looking for God "out there somewhere," you are looking way too far. The kingdom of God is inside you!

Have you ever looked closely at people who spend a lot of time with God? I'm talking about the ones who really know the extreme love and goodness of God to the core of their being. They're filled with a joy that no circumstance seems to be able to touch. They have a calm resolve that their Daddy in heaven is genuinely working everything out in their lives toward a much greater good. They glow with His sweet presence and leak all over the place because they can't help it!

We have many such people in our church, some of whom actually manifest that glory with skin that sparkles with gold, oil that emits from their hands, or a tingling feeling of the intense fire of God just beneath their skin. When you begin to understand that God's glory resides in us all the time, seeing or feeling such displays of wonder are congruent with who God is in us. Those manifestations don't make someone more spiritual or more holy than someone who doesn't experience them. We are spiritual and holy for one reason alone—Christ is in us. But the expressions of Christ in us that show up in astounding ways should cause awe and wonder, not concern.

Through the years, I've been challenged by God to look in the mirror to see what He sees. I'm increasingly stunned when I see the ever-deepening, intense love of Jesus looking back at me. I've had many people tell me they see Jesus looking at them through my eyes.

I carry God's glory. I also release His glory—His immense goodness and loving-kindness—everywhere I go.

And *so do you!*

As a believer, you won't get more glory than you already have, but there's something about knowing what you carry that boosts your child-like exuberance to go release it to the world.

So go take a good, long look in the mirror. But before you do, ask God to help you see what He sees and ask Him, "Show me Your glory."

Put this book down and go to the mirror right now!

How was that? Did you see a glimpse of someone who was greater than you knew before?

Christians often embrace false humility because of the fear of pride. But to know and agree with your greatness is not prideful. Pride boasts that you are great apart from God. Genuine humility knows that your greatness is a gift from the Lord—His greatness in you. On the other end of the spectrum, false humility embraces the lie, "I'm a worm and this is the wretch I will always be." False humility is used by the enemy to keep believers stuck in a pit of hopelessness and mediocrity. Not so for you!

This is the nature of the change that's happening on the earth today. Revival is breaking out across the nations because God is revealing to His children just how great they really are. Revival is God breathing new life into believers so we will accurately represent Him to vast numbers of wayward sons and daughters who are being drawn back home to their loving heavenly Father, who's been awaiting their arrival with arms wide open.

Empowered to Right the Wrongs

By sharing the love of God unapologetically and with power, we are actually undoing the work of the devil, just as Jesus did.[12] Our

Father is really, really good. The devil is really, really bad. Confusion ensues when we get these two facts mixed up. If we don't understand that there is still a battle going on in the earth, even though Jesus has already assured us of the final victory, we can attribute everything that's happening, good and bad, to God.

> It's not rocket science to discern the negative aspects that are destroying people's lives and this earth. We've been deputized to do something about it rather than helplessly standing by, watching the destruction.

Jesus walked the earth making wrong things right by the authority given to Him by His Father. He empowers us to do the same.

> I tell you for certain that if you have faith in me, you will do the same things that I am doing. You will do even greater things, now that I am going back to the Father. Ask me, and I will do whatever you ask. This way the Son will bring honor to the Father. I will do whatever you ask me to do. (John 14:12–14 CEV)

This Scripture became real to me two decades ago when I watched my father-in-law die of a massive heart attack while the paramedics were attempting to revive him. That horrific incident became a catalyst to cause me to assess these words of Jesus. Did He really mean what He said? What did I, as a follower of Jesus, have the authority to do? I went on a several-month journey to discover the answer by looking deeply into the Scriptures, reading many books on healing, and going to numerous conferences. I came away with the only possible conclusion: Jesus meant every word!

Once the Holy Spirit gives us new insight, we become responsible for what we'll do with it. I could have left this new revelation on a shelf to gather dust, but I chose instead to step out and act according to who God said I was. I started out by praying for myself—a safe place to begin!

A year earlier I'd badly injured myself on a backpacking trip where I slipped and gashed my knee on a sharp, jagged rock that cut into my tendons and nerves. It never healed properly and I learned to live with the pain, but I wasn't able to run or do some of the other physical activities I'd previously enjoyed. One day, shortly after coming to the conclusion that I'd been given Jesus' authority to do as He did, I was taking out the garbage, and right in the middle of the parking lot I set the garbage can down and spoke directly to the tendons, nerves, and ligaments in my knee to be healed. I didn't sense any noticeable change after doing so. No fireworks from heaven. No angels shouting, "Hallelujah!"

So I picked up the can and continued on back into my apartment. About fifteen minutes later, I did a set of push-ups and then put weight on my knees to get back up. *Wait a minute,* I thought. *There's no pain in my knee!* With amazement, I put all my weight on the previously injured knee. Still no pain! The next day I ran several miles without pain. That knee's been pain-free ever since!

That was the beginning of a new phase in my journey of representing God's love, sometimes with displays of miraculous power. I've seen hundreds of life-transforming encounters of healing. I've seen an eighty-year-old man paralyzed for six years, because his third, fourth and fifth vertebrae were crushed in an automobile accident, get up and walk! I've seen a teenage girl instantly receive sight in her blind eye! I've seen the deaf hear, cancer disappear, migraines cease, the sense of smell return, blown spinal disks restored to new, diseases and sicknesses such as lupus, Candida, and hepatitis nullified, and much more.

Jesus said, "With God, all things are possible."[13] Part of representing Him accurately is declaring and seeing the possibilities of heaven override the impossibilities of this world.

Probably the major obstacle hindering us from stepping out to declare God's possibilities is fear. What if it doesn't work? What if the person I'm praying for doesn't get healed? I don't have all the answers, but what I do know is that once I believed the words of Jesus and declared healing on His behalf, heaven started breaking in. I've seen undeniable proof of God's powerful and good kingdom making wrongs right again more times than I can remember. I also know that when my genuine motive is love, people feel truly cared for and good things always happen.

> This resurrection life you received from God is not a timid, grave-tending life. It's adventurously expectant, greeting God with a childlike "What's next, Papa?" God's Spirit touches our spirits and confirms who we really are. We know who he is and we know who we are: Father and children."
> (Romans 8:15–16 MSG)

A Life of Integrity

Since we're empowered to represent our Father's exceptionally good heart here on the earth, the integrity of our lives is of utmost importance to God. Fortunately, this doesn't mean God can't or won't use us until our character is perfect; otherwise, none of us would ever get on the playing field. However, developing your character to more clearly display His glory in you is hugely and strategically important to God. So often, we want to charge to the top of the hill, consumed with doing great things for God. He, on the other hand, is consumed with causing us to know who we are and walk accordingly. In fact, when it comes to molding us into the spitting image of His Son, Jesus, He has all the time in the world!

Integrity refers to the state of being whole. It means having the real substance through and through—walking in who you are because you know who you are. Ephesians 4:1 in the Mirror Translation says it like this:

> As one captive in the Lord, I urgently appeal to you therefore, with reference to your original identity, to conduct your life in such a way that your every move bears witness to the weight and value of who you really are.

Paul isn't saying, "Act like a Christian." He's saying, "Know who you are." Your original identity is who God says you are. Paul spent the first three chapters of the book of Ephesians going over your true identity in Christ line by line. Only then does he say, "Now that you know who you really are, be true to your real self."

Paul's saying, "You know that stuff the world is telling you to get messed up with? It has nothing to do with you. You are a person of integrity—that other stuff isn't you."

When we hear God tell us who we are and believe it, our hearts are changed, bringing about integrity in our lives. Just to be clear, integrity isn't trying to be good and having the willpower not to do bad things. Integrity means knowing you were designed for freedom and greatness and you won't settle for less. With this supernatural awareness, you will invite the Holy Spirit to direct your life so you can receive all the benefits of your inheritance, which Jesus paid for on the cross.

> ## Integrity is the natural by-product of knowing you are Christ's presence in this world.

Integrity is the opposite of hypocrisy. The Greek word for hypocrisy in the New Testament also means "an actor."[14] So hypocrisy means, "I'm going to try to act a certain way around you so that you'll think a certain way about me, but it's not who I really am."

Integrity, on the other hand, is you being the real you to the core of your being. The more you know who God says you are and hear it from Him, the more you believe it and agree:

"Wow, I'm really this great! He's made me a person of integrity."

Since this agreement comes by knowing and believing who God says you are, it's imperative that you ask Him often, "Who do You say that I am?" You can't believe old lies about yourself and walk in integrity. The way to battle those lies is to take them straight to Papa and ask Him, "Is this true of me?"

I want to encourage you right now to get out a journal or write in your computer the answer God gives you when you ask Him this question "When You look at me, what do You see?"

Stop right now and ask Him out loud, and wait for His answer to begin entering your thoughts. Hearing God for yourself is transformational!

Write these thoughts down and keep them somewhere that you can review His words to you often. But never tire of asking Him to tell you again. Daddy always has good things to say about you. Always! This is one of the layers behind the meaning of Jesus' words when He said the Father gives us true bread from heaven that we are to eat.[15] Every day you must hear His voice—especially what He thinks about you.

You are "altogether lovely" to your Father.[16] Resting in His delight of you is integral to walking in the true greatness of who you are and not settling for less. This is why I've made His heart for you as crystal clear as I am able. If you need to, go back and reread this book, reminding yourself of the truth of what Papa says about you. Underline phrases that speak to your heart, or put stars in the margin of places where you were filled with the hope of His great love for you—whatever helps you to retrace your steps and remember. Audibly repeat phrases of His heart toward you that bring life and refresh you with joy. The more you hear the Lord tell you Himself what He sees in you, the more you'll walk in it.

> (Pondering the incarnation, the truth about you displayed in Christ) will cause you to be completely reprogrammed in the way you think about yourself! Immerse yourself fully into this God-shaped new man from above! You are created in the image and likeness of God. This is what righteousness and true holiness are all about. (Ephesians 4:23–24 TMT)

You're not going to change yourself for God. Stop that program right this minute. Talk about wasted time and energy on a program that doesn't work! Don't tell God how you're going to change yourself for Him. Instead, determine right now to know who God says you are. When you start thinking about yourself the right way, you'll start living that way. That's the genuine transformation God promised for your life—the one the Holy Spirit is graciously leading you into.

Don't let the world, which doesn't know the first thing about living, tell you what to do. You're way too awesome for that! Hear and agree with your Father, who says to you:

> You're not stuck. You're not drowning. You're not going around the same old mountain again. You're not a broken record. You're My child of purpose and destiny! When I created you, I had a distinct purpose in mind for your life and I'm causing it to happen. It may not always look that way to you, but this is where you must trust Me. What I've prepared for you to do, I'll give you the power and the intention to do. I am leading you in a victory parade of which you are very much a part. You're a victor, not a victim! When I say that I am leading you from glory to glory to glory to glory, that is exactly what I mean. You are moving onward and upward because I have determined it to be so. I want you to thank Me for everything, because there is a much greater plan for your life than you can see in the middle of your circumstances. No matter how big your perceived problems appear to you, I dwarf them with My supreme goodness. No matter what the enemy attempts to do to sidetrack you, My jealous love for you trumps it with ease. No matter how badly you think you've blown it, My grace is enough and you have My permission to proceed with confidence because of Christ, who is in you. All things are working for you, not against you. My Spirit lives in you to assure you of success. I am for you. What else really matters? All of this is true because it is My decision to love you and to help you fulfill the destiny I have for you—and My decision is *final!* I will not change

My mind. I cannot change My mind. You are Mine forever and I wouldn't have it any other way. In case you didn't hear My heart for you loud and clear, I really, really love you![17]

Chapter Reflections

- How can you represent the true heart of your heavenly Father to others in your current life situations?

- How does it feel to know that God calls you His crowning glory and that you were created very good?

- What do you choose to do with God's permission to usher his heavenly kingdom to the earth? What do you think that's supposed to look like?

- Where do you need the Lord's courage to rise up and keep going? Ask for it!

- What did you see when you looked in the mirror and asked God to show you His glory? Write it down in your journal.

- What does hearing Jesus say that you'll do even greater things than Him do to you? What areas of your authority in Christ do you want to pursue further?

- Are there ways in which you are trying to act like a Christian instead of living true to who God says you are? Where do you need God to refresh your way of thinking about yourself?

Chapter 11

Love Always Wins

த

*I trust you to represent My heart of love
to a world full of people
desperately needing My affection and approval.
That's one of the many reasons I will never stop
pouring out My love upon you, My child.
What you receive from Me—go give it away!*

Bob Jones, a fatherly prophetic voice to this generation, shared a story at a conference that I've never forgotten. He died and went to heaven and there he saw Jesus, who eventually sent him back into his body on this earth to finish what God had sent him here to accomplish. But when Bob met Jesus in heaven, the Lord asked him one question: "Did you learn to love?"

Did You Learn to Love?

It wasn't "Did you tell people about Me?" or "Did you worship Me?" or "Did you use the gifts I gave you wisely?"—although these are great things to do.

No, Jesus asked Bob, "Did you learn to love?"

Jesus gave His followers a new command on the night of His arrest—an exclamation point to His ministry on the earth. He said, "Love one another. As I have loved you, so you must love one another" (John 13:34 NIV). This was the essence of the new covenant of grace. *I will love you first—unconditionally, wholeheartedly, unreservedly—so that you can allow that very same love to pour forth through you to one another.*

This is how the apostle Paul describes that covenant love:

> Love (the revealed value that God sees in every man) gives truth its voice. In this atmosphere of love, spontaneous growth is inevitable. The whole person is addressed in Christ, who is the head of the body; He is the conclusion of the conversation. From Him flows the original composition and detail of our design like words intertwined in poetry, (like a conductor of music, *epichoregeo*) they connect layer upon layer to complete the harmony, following the rhythm of His thoughts like footprints. Meanwhile, the body thrives and pulsates with the energy of love. Each individual part (portion) finds its full measure there. (Ephesians 4:15–16 TMT)

The simple truth is that love changes people! When we finally accept and receive the superabundant love and acceptance of our Papa in heaven, we are forever transformed. And when we freely give away to others what we have freely received, they are changed too.

A Baptism of Love

At a leadership gathering of my church during a very intimate time of worship, I was taken in a vision to the throne room of God. I saw the twenty-four elders around the throne, worshipping Jesus. Then I looked directly into the eyes of Jesus! My first reaction was one of unworthiness to be in His beautiful, breathtaking presence. I knelt down and placed a crown that had been on my head before Him on the ground. Jesus came toward me, took my hand, and raised me up, placing the crown back on my head. I was stunned by this gesture of overwhelming grace and kindness. He said, "I'm going to allow you to see people the way I do, in a much truer light than you've ever seen before." At that moment, I felt as though I was receiving a baptism of love that washed over me and transformed my ability to see with love in a much greater capacity.

Back from the vision, I read to the group of leaders the love passage from 1 Corinthians 13:4–8 (in Barclay's New Testament). I was so deeply moved by the vision I'd just experienced and the extravagant love of my Savior, Jesus, I could only get a few words out at a time before deeply sobbing. I didn't want to cry like a baby in front of my friends, but I was unable to contain my emotions in such a holy moment. So I would collect myself the best I could and get a few more words out before sobbing again. This is what I read bit by bit:

> Love is patient with people. Love is kind.
>
> There is no envy in love;
>> there are no proud claims;
>> there is no conceit.
>
> Love never does the graceless thing;
>> never insists on its rights,
>> never irritably loses its temper;
>> never nurses its wrath to keep it warm.
>
> Love finds nothing to be glad about
>> when someone goes wrong,
>> but it is glad when truth is glad.
>
> Love can stand any kind of treatment;
>> love's first instinct is to believe in people;
>> love never regards anyone or anything as hopeless;
>> nothing can happen that can break love's spirit.
>
> Love lasts forever.

Love always wins! If you continually choose to love someone, eventually it has a noticeable impact on him or her, because love is the greatest change agent on the earth. It's one of three things that the Bible says remains forever.

That's right, there are three things you get to take with you from this world to heaven. They are faith, hope, and love.

But far and away, the greatest of the three is love. That means any love you express toward another is never wasted!

Without Love, What's the Point?

The well-known description of love in 1 Corinthians 13 follows a description of the amazingly powerful gifts that the Holy Spirit has given to believers. Paul explains that if we use those gifts of power without love, even with the best of intentions, it's like a loud, clanging cymbal.

I played the French horn in an orchestra for years, and let me tell you, cymbals are astonishingly loud and jarring. A cymbal played with a full orchestra at just the right time in a movement can be exhilarating. But if you were talking with someone at a coffee shop and someone were to suddenly crash a cymbal right next to you, it would rattle your nervous system to the core. It would be unnerving, not comforting. It would be harsh, not pleasurable. That's how using the gifts of the Spirit without genuine, caring love would feel. If we don't have the tenderheartedness of our Father toward the ones we are approaching, we can do much more harm than good.

Here's Peter's take on the same concept:

> Above all, preserve an intense love for each other, since love covers over many a sin. (First Peter 4:8 NJB)

Peter emphasizes, "Above all." He's saying, "If you don't get anything else I'm saying, guard this place of intense love for each other." Love is the one thing the enemy has no ammunition against. How can he fight love? In an atmosphere where the love of the Father is understood and experienced, you will see a lot of really happy people! If we lived in the reality of the Father's love all the time, there would be continual joy.

What Happens in an Atmosphere of Grace and Love

People long to be loved and they long for their lives to mean something. Experiencing the Father's deep love for you will accomplish both. Once you rest in the extravagant goodness of God, your life will bear unimaginable fruit for the kingdom. A life that is at rest in Papa's love will supernaturally pour out what He so lavishly pours in.

Over the years I have watched love cause inevitable spontaneous growth in one person after another. I marvel as people come to Blazing Fire Church for the first time, often broken and hurting, and are transformed by the love and acceptance they encounter from others who themselves have been transformed by the Father's love.

People who have been stuck for decades have been rapidly transformed with heavy doses of the unchanging truth of Papa's affection. A constant atmosphere of grace and love changes people.

Becky was a student at Blazing Fire Church's Kingdom Training School of Supernatural Ministry. She began the school shattered by a lifetime of pain and lies that had created a debilitating stranglehold on her. Although she had experienced degrees of healing along the way from a God who continually lifted her out of a pit of despair, the nine months of school where she continuously soaked in the truth of her heavenly Father's affection and acceptance became a major turning point in her healing. Here's the creative and moving narrative of that transformation as told in story form by Becky herself:

> Once upon a time, a beautiful baby girl was born into a broken, unhappy family. The family wanted to love her, care for her, and help her grow, but what happened instead—because the family didn't know how to love—was pain, heartache, and torment. During her life, in times of distress, there was a Presence that cared for and comforted the child. She rarely saw it. She never felt it because she

had lost her ability to feel. She hid away in shell-armor so thick that no earthly force could possibly break through. All she knew was the pain she nursed inside her shell. And it continued. Endlessly.

New pain—the type she understood—was allowed, but tenderness, hope, and love were seen as damaging. They exposed the tender, hurting areas of her soul to a painful shower of love, and she couldn't bear that kind of pain. Still, the Presence persisted, brooding over His hurting child. He quietly, gently caressed her heart inside the shell and dulled the sharp edges of her many wounds. He loosed her grip on the repetitious recounting of her despair. He took her through things that led to more healing, this time with other people involved. Sometimes, the healing hurt. Mostly, it helped.

But still the thorns of torment encircled her mind. The quietness of her heart still resounded with the screams of herself as a little girl. She struggled hopelessly to break free of the hard shell-prison she had put around herself, but no one could hear her cries except the Presence.

Gradually, the shell weakened. The tender affections of the One who loved her touched her mind and showed her peace. For a moment, the torment stopped. When the torment resumed, she pursued the peace with all her heart. It was a moment of life she had never known before. Earlier, she had given up and given her life to her Creator, hoping for death. Now she gave her life to her Creator, hoping for life.

The Creator answered her cries for peace. Slowly, as internal peace made its way into her heart, an external peace started to show. This peace led the way to other gifts the Creator knew she was ready to experience.

One beautiful day, joy embraced her. Her heart was happy in a way she had never experienced before. She reveled in her day of happiness, hoping it would never end. When the day came to a close, as all days do, she tucked that memory away in a special place in her heart. Hope started to grow. She began to crave the joy. Gradually, more joy was added. The joy was breaking something hard and ugly in her heart and mind.

On another day, someone showed her a moment of love. The person looked into her eyes, saw her, and smiled. There was a sincere welcome—an openness she had never seen before. This was a new thing. In her world of self-preservation and bitterness, rejection was normal. To be welcome, without having to do anything to impress someone ... that was unheard of.

She started to talk to her Creator about love, and the love lessons began. She started to crave love. She learned to love her Creator. Learned to love things. She even learned to extend the selfless love she was given, but she still hated herself. She saw herself as ugly, something to despise. Despair would grip her heart often.

Her Creator started showing her that she was beautiful, that He made her to be lovely, sweet, and kind. He showed her that she was good, not an evil thing to be tolerated. As she grew to accept this, her hard shell cracked. Feelings that she had tried to kill came back. Love seeped its way deeper into her heart, exposing the bitterness and anger that still raged through the deepest wounds in her soul. "Mercy!" she cried to her Creator. He heard. And answered. He healed. And He laughed with joy.

As the healing progressed, the prison-shell fell completely away. The Creator was now her dearest friend, who loved her unconditionally. His amazing love had redefined who she was by changing her outlook, changing her speech, changing her. A shift had occurred. She found a new ability to extend this love to others, to share her heart, share her emotions. Those feelings, once a source of great pain, were now a place of abiding joy.

Despair fled and was no more.

Over the years I've discovered an amazing, freeing truth about my role as a pastor. Trying to run people's lives and tell them what to do simply doesn't work. My job is not to fix people or try to change them. I can't do it!

> My job is to tell people what God thinks of them and how amazing they are, until they believe it.

The better grasp I have on how much my Father adores me as His son, the greater my capacity is to tell people what God thinks about them and how astounding they are in Christ. Once they get it, they begin to soar into their destinies as they were created to do, no longer bound by the chains of legalism and the self-condemnation and self-hatred that legalism brings.

The more pain that someone has experienced in life, the longer it usually takes for the ice to melt or the heartache to dissipate, but it's only a matter of time before love wins out. Whether or not you are a pastor, you have the ability every day of your life to bring hope to people just by sharing the powerful simplicity of a Father who longs for His kids with every ounce of His being.

> Watch what God does, and then you do it. … Mostly what God does is love you. (Ephesians 5:1 MSG)

Using our Words to Bring Life

Jesus is our perfect model for what life in the new covenant should look like. If we can see how Jesus loves, we can ask the Holy Spirit to empower us to love the same way. In order to take a deeper look into the heart of Jesus, let's look at how He treats His bride, who is the Church—all the believers across the globe, past, present, and future.

The husband provides leadership to his wife the way Christ does to his church, not by domineering but by cherishing. … Husbands, go all out in your love for your wives, exactly as Christ did for the church—a love marked by giving, not getting. Christ's love makes the church whole. His words evoke her beauty. Everything he does and says is designed to bring the best out of her, dressing her in dazzling white silk, radiant with holiness. And that is how husbands ought to love their wives. They're really doing themselves a favor—since they're already "one" in marriage. No one abuses his own body, does he? No, he feeds and pampers it. That's how Christ treats us, the Church, since we are part of his body. (Ephesians 5:25–30 MSG)

While this is excellent counsel for any husband who wants to be married to a princess (since you'll most certainly have a princess if you treat her as one), I'm using this passage to illustrate Jesus' astounding ability to love.

Jesus continually speaks words of affirmation and encouragement and love to you, evoking your beauty, because you and Jesus are *one.* So whatever He does to you, He is doing to Himself.

Think about it.

Jesus will never speak words to tear you down or degrade you in any way because He would be bringing Himself down with you.

What He does to you He is doing to Himself, because the moment you said yes to Jesus, you were eternally joined with Him in a love covenant that has no end.

This is why Paul says in Romans 8 that the only one who has the power to judge you is the One who died for you—Jesus—and He is completely and in every way *for* you. This is also why Paul says in 2

Timothy 2:13, "If we are faithless, He is faithful still, for He cannot disown His own self."

He is infinitely patient with us and He continues to treasure us because, above all, He must be faithful to Himself. Besides, Jesus doesn't want a dejected, depressed bride.

He wants a bride who is radiant with beauty. Therefore, He is going to speak the truth of our beauty and our greatness until we get it, so that we will be the glowing, love-soaked bride He earnestly desires to have by His side.

And Jesus says, "As I have loved you, this is the way you are to love one another, never tearing others down, because you are one with Me and with one another."

Sharing the Right Message

How is it that any one of us has come to know God? Was it because we were so clever in figuring it out? Or was it because He first demonstrated His love, kindness, and mercy to us, and we responded to Him?

> The wonder of love is not that we loved God, but that He first loved us enough to send His Son to remove the barrier that our sins had erected between us and him. (1 John 4:10 BNT)

Every one of us came to Him because He sovereignly touched our hearts in a way that we could not deny. God broke through our walls of pain, defenses, or indifference. He made Himself irresistible, offering us the love, forgiveness, and acceptance we desperately needed.

> Surely, Yahweh's mercies are not over, his deeds of faithful love not exhausted; every morning they are renewed; great is his faithfulness! (Lamentations 3:22–23 NJB)

When we represent God to people as His ambassadors, we have to have the right message. God already accepts His children—all of them. He accepted us long before we recognized His love and took Him up on His offer of spending eternity with Him.

We have made reaching out to people way too complicated. God's evangelism strategy is simple. Jesus explained it this way:

> "Let anyone who is thirsty come to me! Let anyone who believes in me come and drink! As Scripture says, 'From his heart shall flow streams of living water.'" (John 7:37–38 NJB)

We are to be so filled with the Holy Spirit, so filled with the resurrection power of Jesus, and so filled with the love of the Father that it gushes out of us—the transformational presence of God effortlessly overflowing to the world around us. Jesus said to His followers, "Freely you have received; freely give."[1]

Therefore, the key is not so much in the giving away as it is in being a proficient receiver, because we can't give away what we don't have.

Once we experience the extravagant love of God, we'll have all that we need and more to love others in a way that is genuinely supernatural. In a filled place, God will use us to bring life and hope and refreshment to those who are dry and desperate for the living God.

Some Christians seem to believe that it is their job to tell others how sinful they are and to warn them about the impending hell they will face because they're not living according to God's standards. There is a fundamental flaw to this approach. The job of making one's need for a Savior obvious because of the sin condition we're all born with belongs solely to the Holy Spirit. His role is described by Jesus in John 16:7–11 (TSNT):

> I'm telling you the truth: it is for your benefit that I'm going away. If I didn't go away, the One who is called to your side

to help and encourage wouldn't come to you. Since I am going, I will send him to you. And when he comes, he will convince the world of the truth about sin, and about being made right with God, and about judgment. About sin, because they don't believe me, and also about being made right with God, because I'm going to the Father where you'll no longer see me, and also about judgment, because the ruler of this world now stands judged.

I've watched with great sadness as well-intentioned but angry Christians have gone to organizations or mass celebrations where they disagreed with the choices people were making, only to shout out horrendous lies like "God hates you!"—followed by the description of how hot the flames are in the hell God is sending them to. In all my days, I've yet to see a single harassed, hated individual stop and say, "Oh, I see the truth now. Thank you. Tell me how I can know this God of yours who hates me."

If you have been on the receiving end of such hateful statements from Christians, I sincerely and humbly ask for your forgiveness on behalf of those who have hurt you. Any form of hatred intended to bring shame and condemnation, rather than restoration and freedom, do not originate from Papa's heart. Release the pain and continue your journey of intimacy with the One who loves you and receives you as His beloved child.

Believe it or not, most people—believers and prebelievers alike—are well aware of their shortcomings. Somewhere inside them, they know they need a hero, a Savior, to come and do for them what they can't do for themselves. The piece they are missing, and what they desperately need to know, is that there is a Father who made them, who knows them better than they know themselves, who wants them with all of His heart, and who doesn't count their sins against them. They won't trust a God who's depicted as furious, hateful, and full of rage. How can they? Who would come running to that kind of a father? That's the type of father many broken people had to endure the abuses of, or chose to run far away from just as soon as they were able.

> We're doing no one a favor by falsely representing our loving Papa as a hater who is opening the doors of hell to throw His children into.

In fact, once, when Jesus wasn't being received well, His disciples asked Him, "Should we call down fire on them?"[2] They had a good reason for asking that, because there was a precedent for it in the Scriptures, about which they would have known. Remember Elijah calling down fire on the prophets of Baal?[3] The disciples were probably thinking that they were stepping out with great courage and faith to do what a mighty prophet in the Scriptures had done before them. Jesus' response shocked them to the core.

> He turned and rebuked and severely censured them. He said, "You do not know of what sort of spirit you are. For the Son of Man did not come to destroy men's lives, but to save them." (Luke 9:55–56 AMP)

As we learned in Chapter 10, the role we're given by God is ambassadors of reconciliation. We are to take the hands of sons and daughters and lead them to the outstretched arms of Papa God. It is our greatest and highest privilege to share this profoundly life-changing truth with people.

As you feed yourself on the Father's love, His pleasure for you, and His kindness, mercy, and gentleness toward you, you will impact those whom He sends along your path. This plan of Christ in you and through you is so simple that we can easily overlook it and replace it with our attempts to appease God by reaching out to others. God doesn't need appeasing—Jesus took care of that one *fully* on the cross.

> God wants lovers who gush ... drinkers of Him who
> leak ... filled vessels of glory who spill ... children
> of Light who shine like stars in the universe!

Every Person Has Infinite Value

One of the amazing privileges I've had is to go out with other believers to the streets of San Francisco late at night to bring a warm meal and a kind word of God's love and acceptance to the homeless who are huddled in doorways or along back alleys. One particularly impactful experience for me occurred on my very first venture out. Feeling somewhat unsure of ourselves, our group approached several homeless men who were sheltered in the entryway of a store long after closing time, the smell of urine lingering. The men were jovial with us, clinging to their alcoholic beverages of choice concealed in crinkled-up brown paper bags. We handed out prepared meals to the grateful men. While pouring out a cup of hot coffee to an outstretched trembling hand, I was suddenly drawn to the side, where another of their group was lying flat on the ground, intoxicated beyond the ability to sit up or stand with his friends.

I approached him, knelt down to be close to his face, and asked, "Do you want something to eat?" His closed eyes flickered open for a moment, attempting to focus on the face of this unfamiliar voice that was addressing him. Without uttering a word, his eyes closed again and he retreated to his inebriated, semi-conscious state. Undeterred and filled with an inexpressible compassion for this young man, I leaned in closer and said in a soft and warm tone, "You have a Father in heaven who loves you with all His heart."

I wondered if my words were registering with this man in his present condition, but I continued. "God hasn't forgotten you. He's with you all the time and He is always for you." Still no response or acknowledgement of my affirming words. Yet somehow I knew that my voice of hope was not falling on deaf ears. "He's so proud to call you His son," I told him. In that instant a tear welled up in his eyes and rolled down his cheek. He opened his eyes again, this time with more clarity, and looked directly into my eyes with an expression of shame mixed with hope.

I could almost hear his thoughts pleading, *Could this possibly be true?*

Peering into his precious soul through the gateway of his eyes, I reiterated the truth of the Father's acceptance and approval. He never actually spoke a word to me, but his eyes communicated his sincere gratitude, and there was a glimmer of hope that had not been present before. I prayed a blessing of peace over his heart before our team continued on in our journey to encounter others who needed food for their stomachs and hope for their souls. I will probably never know on this side of heaven what impact those words of the Father's love and acceptance had on that young man, but I know they weren't wasted.

Love is never wasted, because love always wins!

Our Papa of love says:

> Rain and snow fall from the sky. But they don't return without watering the earth that produces seeds to plant and grain to eat. That's how it is with my words. They don't return to me without doing everything I send them to do. (Isaiah 55:10–11 CEV)

No More Judgment

It wasn't my job to try to fix that homeless man or to tell him what big mistakes he was making in his life.

> You, therefore, have no excuse, you who pass judgment on someone else, for at whatever point you judge the other, you are condemning yourself, because you who pass judgment do the same things. (Romans 2:1 NIV)

We are no different from this young man in that "while we were still sinners, Christ died for us."[4] We would've had no ability to find God except that He first came and got us with tenderness and compassion.

> When we choose to judge someone instead of extending the Father's love and mercy, we disqualify ourselves from being able to reach that person.

God will use another to do so unless, of course, we're able to see what spirit is in operation and choose to turn back to Christ's spirit of love. Our job is to love people and to provide the hope that comes when we share the truth of God's heart with them.

When the religious leaders of His day approached Jesus, bringing with them a woman they'd caught in adultery, they were trying to trap Jesus by asking what they should do. They knew very well the Law demanded that she be stoned to death. Jesus replied:

> If any one of you is without sin, let him be the first to throw a stone at her. (John 8:7 NIV)

The oldest and the wisest ones were the first to leave until the entire crowd was gone and it was only Jesus and the woman—Jesus who had never sinned in His life and a woman in deep shame from being caught in the act of having sex with a married man. (You should rightly ask where that man was who got caught with her and who is mysteriously missing … but that's another matter for another time.) Jesus' response tells us much about His heart and the heart of His Father.

> Has no one condemned you? Then neither do I condemn you. Go now and leave your life of sin. (John 8:10–11 NIV)

Jesus was saying to her, "I've come for the very purpose of showing you the heart of the Father, who forgives His children. What you did isn't the real you. Choose to live as the princess you truly are."

Jesus reflects the heart of our Father, who encourages us to continue reaching out to the hurting ones who don't know their true identity.

> My word will once again be heard in the streets and on street corners. But this time it will reflect My heart. It will not be shouts of fear or judgment, but of My mercy and My love. Do not hold back just because it was done wrongly in previous times. Be My voice, be My ambassadors of love to the world. I am coming in power. You will see signs and wonders on the earth unlike anything you've seen yet. My love will heal wounded hearts like never before. Don't underestimate the power of your voice that calls to the lost, the hurting, and the broken. Declare life![5]

Love and Power

Jesus told us that signs and wonders would take place in the lives of those who believe.[6] People are searching for something that's real. There are times when the power of God makes His love tangible in a way that's undeniable. Just remember that love is what people are aching for most of all, even in the midst of powerful miracles.

While I was ministering in Brazil, a forlorn teenager by the name of Teresa came up to receive prayer. I learned from this young woman that her parents had gone through a particularly traumatic divorce and she had been struggling with deep depression ever since. With obvious shame, Teresa recounted how in her depressed state of anxiety she repeatedly ripped out all of her eyelashes and eyebrow hairs. Her eyelashes grew back, but her eyebrows eventually did not anymore because of the scarring her eyebrow follicles had endured with the continued self-abuse. Because of the embarrassment that this condition caused her, Teresa's sad eyes barely mustered a glance toward my compassionate gaze. She was asking for a miracle of the restoration of her eyebrows, but her much deeper, hidden need was the restoration of her soul. She was clearly struggling with self-hatred and shame. Looking at Teresa, all I could feel was the Father's overwhelming love and approval for His precious daughter.

I looked deep into her eyes and tenderly declared the love of her heavenly Papa. "Teresa, your Father in heaven loves you with all of His heart. He says to you, 'You are my beloved daughter and I am very pleased with you.'" Warm tears cascaded down her face.

"You are My special princess—Daddy's girl! And nothing you do or don't do will ever change My deep affection for you. You are everything I've ever wanted. You make Me happy, Teresa!" Her countenance softened as she latched onto the words of life that were ringing true in her ears.

After affirming her position in the Father's heart, I proceeded, using my rightful authority in Christ to declare a creative miracle of perfectly restored hair follicles and rapid growth of her eyebrows. I had no idea how rapidly the Lord would do it.

Teresa was one of the last people I prayed for that night, at about midnight. Our team came back at eight o'clock the next morning to continue teaching at the conference we were hosting. As I entered the church building, I heard a joy-filled squeal from across the room. Teresa, wildly waving her arms, bounded toward me with a huge smile on her face. Now *this* was the true daughter of the King!

After stopping in front of me and pointing excitedly to her eyebrows, she cried, "Look, Pastor Brent!"

I peered in closer, and there was a quarter of an inch of hair stubble growing throughout both eyebrows! That was an undeniable supernatural touch from God to heal Teresa in the physical realm. More important, it was exactly what this princess needed to assure her of the love that was proclaimed over her just eight hours previously.

I believe it's the greatest honor and highest privilege to accurately represent the genuine heart of the Father to His sons and daughters on the earth.

> This is what true ministry is all about. It is
> giving away the love you've received from
> God, however He has wired you to do it.

Anything else leads us back to performance—trying to do something for God, hoping He will approve and be happier with us because of our efforts. Remember, you please Him because you are His—Jesus has taken care of the performance part for you. Your life is a fragrant offering to the Lord. He pours into you, and you pour out. That's what you were born to do!

> Mimic God; you are His offspring. This is how, let love be your life; equal to the love of Christ in the way He abandoned Himself to us. His love is contagious, not reluctant but extravagant. Sacrificial love pleases God like the sweet aroma of worship. (Ephesians 5:1–2 TMT)

You're Making a Difference

If you're tempted to believe that you're not making a difference in this world, I want to offer you heaven's perspective. Every single time you share some of the Father's love that's in your heart with a person, you are making a huge difference.

> Every smile, every kind word, every act of forgive-
> ness and mercy you display toward someone not
> only affects that person's life, but is used by God in
> a kingdom ripple effect that goes around the world.
> That makes you a genuine world changer!

> This is the time of Jesus, the Liberator, and religious rules aren't what counts—not now, no, all that stuff is old currency. The only things that register on God's scoreboard are taking God at his word and loving people. ... You were

picked to be free. But it's not a "license to kill" (or whatever else the Old You fancies doing)—no, it's a freedom to work for other people's benefit 'cos you love them. (Galatians 5:6, 13 *The Word on the Street*)

That last line about working for other people's benefit because you love them is a great definition of covenant love. Covenant love says, "I'm in this for your best!" That's God's promise to you for all time. And that's why you have the capacity to do the same for others.

So what we really need is a whole lot more revelation and experience of the endless incoming supply of God's love, so that we can endlessly give it away to everyone we meet.

This is exactly what Paul was praying would happen to us.

I'm asking him to dig into his incredible wealth and increase your supplies of his Spirit's supernatural power flowing direct into your core. ... I'm asking that you'll plug into the Liberator's love and be able to get your head (and heart) 'round its dimensions: the size, scale, depth, density, scope, range and texture of this love are beyond quantum physics; they can't be squeezed into some formula—they're impossible to measure. But by trying, you'll expand your capacity and will have more space for God to fill—his love supplies won't run short! (Ephesians 3:15–19 *The Word on the Street*)

Be at peace as God's presence flows directly into your core. Papa is on your side and His extravagant love for you is working right through you to make a huge difference in this world ... one heart at a time.

The antidote to discouragement is Daddy's approval, which you have! The antidote to weariness is to rest in His gracious, loving arms, which is your forever inheritance that you get to enjoy now. The antidote to hopelessness is His assurance that He will complete all that He has begun in you—and He will!

You are chosen, loved, wanted, blessed, favored, cherished, adored, cared for, esteemed, highly valued, treasured, desired, and given inestimable worth by God.

He says to you, "Keep giving away My love. You're doing better than you think!"

Chapter Reflections

- How would you respond if the Lord asked you today, "Did you learn to love?"

- Knowing that love is never wasted, how can you reach out to someone with love today?

- Where have you judged another recently instead of offering hope? If possible, how can you make it right with this person?

- Ask God to put someone before you today who needs to hear the good news of His love and acceptance.

- How have you made a difference as a world changer today with a simple act of love?

Chapter 12

The Father's Blessing

❧

I magine that you are Adam. (You remember, the guy God created so He could be a father—so He would have someone to lavish His love on? Yeah, that's the one.)

Okay, so you're Adam, having just been created. You got your body, your brain, your emotions, your desire and creativity (because you're made in His likeness). What's left? Ah, yes. Your eyes are still shut. There's no breathing going on yet. God is about to breathe life into you.

He comes close ... closer still ... face-to-face with you. Ahhhhhh, the breath of heaven now fills your lungs. Your eyes open for the very first time. Papa's right there, giving you breath.

What's the first thing you see? What look does He have on His face? (Would it be a look of disappointment? One of anger? Not a chance!) Just imagine the look He has as He gazes upon you. It's love. Affection. Amazement. Tenderness. Wonder!

This is the first thing Adam saw.

And He's still looking at us like that!

His Affectionate Gaze

Long, long ago, your forever Father wanted you to exist so that He would have you to lavish His love on. And long, long ago, your forever Father planted a dream inside of you that would be fulfilled in the time when He determined you would be born and walk on the earth. His dream is unique in each child, but every dream contains the same component of enjoying greater and greater intimacy with Him and displaying His glorious presence with all those with whom you come into contact. What that looks like is completely unique to each of us. Discover with God the voice He's given you to make a difference in this world. Then, release it with all you've got!

As you continue on this journey of life with your Father, here are a few reminders from His heart He wants you to remember:

I'm not putting up with you and I'm not put off by you. I'm captivated, enamored, fascinated, and smitten with you.

Because I'm fully committed to you, I'm positioning you for success, even using what you would think are failures to launch you into the destiny I've designed for you.

I do not see "character flaws" in you; I see the splendor of My perfect creation when I look at you. I am lovingly removing anything that would dim the light of My glory through you.

While some would say there are no superstars, I want to remind you that My Son, Jesus, is the never-ending Supernova exploding from within you, making you an infinitely bright star in a galaxy of like-shining stars. As you display My light and life and freely give it away to others, you bring Me great joy and delight.

And never forget that I love you this very moment and every moment of our forever lives together.

Can Daddy's love really be as good as what I've described in this book? Actually, it's far better than anything I could possibly describe using mere words. But it's the best I can do to convey a heart that is kinder, gentler, more compassionate, and more merciful than we can come close to comprehending. Allow yourself to believe wholeheartedly: "It's true! My Father's heart is this good and then some!"

> You'll have all eternity to explore the vastness and yumminess of God's all-consuming love for you, but go ahead and plunge as deep as you can right here in this life.

Ask God for His help—that's what He loves to do!

His Banner over You Is Love

When the Lord says to you, "I've brought you to My banqueting table and My banner over you is love,"[1] He is saying so much more than "I got a great meal for you with a big sign posted over your head." You see, it's not actually a banquet table, but more literally a house of wine.[2] And the banner is not a sign, it is a huge flag that is hoisted and wildly waved as a sign of victory and triumph.

So look at it this way. God ushers you into the deepest places of intimacy with Him. As you are toasting to your everlasting relationship together, He breaks out the biggest, most glorious flag you have ever seen, because He can't help Himself! The love-embroidered flag is leaving splashes of His glory as it rips through the air, trumpeting the finality of your love relationship with Him that has been sealed forever because of the victory of Jesus on the cross!

He is beside Himself with joy and laughter, reveling in the unchangeable status of you and Him, together engaged in an eternal gaze of mutual adoration! Lest you think I am stretching the truth, remember His words to you:

> You are wholly beautiful, My beloved, and without a blemish.
> … you ravish My heart with a single one of your glances.
> (Song of Songs 4:7, 9 NJB)

How is it possible that He sees you without a blemish? With great joy I remind you that Jesus loves the Church, His bride, and "gave Himself up for her so that He might sanctify her, having cleansed her by the washing of water with the word, that He might present to Himself the church in all her glory, having no spot or wrinkle or any such thing; but that she would be holy and blameless!" (Ephesians 5:25–27 NASB)

When you know you're treasured like this, you feel lovable and look radiant! Those who know the extreme joy of belonging to God and who are convinced they're loved by Him are going to be the most influential people in history in these last days.

At the beginning of this book, we saw how experiencing genuine encounters of God's love is essential to transform us. My earnest prayer for each one of you reading this book is that you have become convinced of your heavenly Father's love for you in a way that goes far beyond anything you've known before. I also pray you've now had several real encounters on the way to a lifetime of experiencing His tender love for you.

It's not enough to simply know as a cerebral fact that God loves you. Daddy invites you every day of your life into encounters with Him in which His heart and yours are entwined in a tangible way.

I understand our Christian life is not dependant solely upon feelings. On the other hand, a love relationship where feelings don't exist doesn't make any sense whatsoever.

I encourage you to continue saying out loud, "Daddy, You love me!" until it becomes a reality for you. Even if you're not feeling it yet, the truth will penetrate deep into your heart until one day you realize that His love is more real to you than anything else in this life. And no one will be able to persuade you otherwise. Keep going on this journey of friendship and intimacy with God.

Receiving the Father's Blessing

Every person on this earth is hungering for a true blessing from the Father. This Father's blessing, which you are about to receive, is real. And it's for you. Read it out loud and agree with it as many times and for as long as it takes to believe it. Receiving your Father's blessing to the core of your being will change your life forever!

Hear God saying these words to you:

> My amazing son, My precious daughter, you are My beloved child in whom I am so pleased! I am your Father who adores you. I love you! I've always loved you. I don't love you because of what you can do for me. I love you because you are Mine—not for any other reason. You are Mine! I love you with a passionate, strong, and immovable love and I will never ever change My mind.
>
> I not only love you, but I really, really like you! I like what I made. I like who you are. When I made you, you were my dream fulfilled. I delight in you. I celebrate you. I dance over you and sing My songs of pleasure over you. I'm very, very proud of you. I'm thrilled to call you Mine. You're doing so well! You're doing so much better than you think you are. Keep going, My child! And I want you to know that you measure up. You are enough. Even if others have told you otherwise, My voice of truth is the only voice that matters. And I think you are absolutely astounding. You're My success story. I'm not done yet! Just watch what I do with your life.

My child, I bless you—not reluctantly, but wholeheartedly. I give to you My Father's blessing! It's My heart's desire to bless you. So I bless you with My favor. I bless you with My goodness. I bless you with My grace. I bless you with My peace. And I bless you with My joy.

I bless you with the full inheritance of My kingdom that's yours through My Son, Jesus. Everything that's Mine is yours! I hold nothing back from you, because you are Mine. You are My chosen prince, My chosen princess, with full access to My kingdom. My royalty is in your blood!

I want you to know that I'm on your side, no matter what. I'm totally for you—always. I want you with all of My heart, and I will have you as My very own forever. My beloved child, My heart is your home. Enter into the joy of My heart and My kingdom. Not someday, but right now![3]

Because agreement is essential for your heart to receive the truth, I invite you to speak aloud these words back to your heavenly Father, who's listening with great happiness:

Daddy, I agree! I'm your child—your son/daughter and your prince/princess.

I receive Your great big love for me and I say to You in return, "I love You with all my heart!"

I realize that by expressing my love for you, I've turned Your heart inside out. Somehow I have the unique ability to bring immense joy to You in a way no one else can.

I agree I don't have to do a single thing to bring You that pleasure, but You are pleased with me because I'm Yours.

I'm blessed and highly favored as Your child of promise—living in the extravagant grace of the new covenant—my free gift in Christ.

You've put Your Spirit inside me to guide me, comfort me, and assure me of victory and success. I am never alone.

You are always for me—never against me.

You delight in me.

You like me.

What's Yours is mine.

I will never again have to work for what is already mine—especially Your approval and Your love.

I am loved beyond measure.

Thank you, Daddy!

Feel free to add anything else you want to say. He loves to hear the sound of your sweet voice.

I bless you on your continued journey into the depths of the Father's heart. I assure you it's only going to get better from here. Your Father's going to make certain of that!

Chapter Reflections

- Go back over the words in this book that came alive to you—the places where you cried and the places where you laughed with joy. If you need to, mark the places of significance for you to easily find and saturate yourself in truth. Then keep writing your thoughts in a journal, because Papa will most certainly speak to you. Once you know His true character, any lies will be clearly seen for what they are and dismissed as quickly as they come.

- In what ways can you release the Father's blessing to others?

Endnotes

Chapter 1: A Father Who Loves You with All His Heart

1 Romans 8:15.

2 For further information, read "The Primacy of Human Touch" by Ben Benjamin, PhD, and Ruth Werner, LMT, H-E-A-L-T-H Touch News (http://www.benbenjamin.com/pdfs/Issue2.pdf).

3 John 3:7.

4 1 John 4:16.

Chapter 2: A Father Unlike Any Other

1 You can read all about this direct connection with your spirit and God's Spirit in 1 Corinthians 2:9–16.

2 Romans 8:38–39.

3 Colossians 2:15.

4 Romans 8:28.

5 If you need help to heal in these areas, here are some helpful resources: *Redeeming the Past: Recovering from the Memories that Cause our Pain* by David Seamands, *Healing for Damaged Emotions* by David Seamands, and *The Life Model: Living from the Heart Jesus Gave You* by Friesen, Wilder, Bierling, Koepcke, and Poole.

6 These statements of Papa's love and care for you were taken from Hebrews 13:5, 1 John 3:1, Hosea 2:14, Hebrews 12:7, 10, and Isaiah 43:1.

7 Luke 23:34, KJV

8 Matthew 10:8, NLT

9 Luke 1:37; Philippians 4:13.

10 Malachi 4:6.

Chapter 3: A Father Who Likes You and Wants You

1 2 Peter 3:9.

2 Revelation 3:5.

3 John 14:6.

4 Colossians 1:15.

5 Hebrews 12:23.

6   Luke 15:8–10.

7   Revelation 1:14; 2:18; 19:12.

8   1 Peter 1:18–19.

Chapter 4: A Father Who Celebrates You

1   Hebrews 12:2, NIV.

2   Psalm 139:17–18.

3   See John 3:35.

4   See Song of Songs 6:3, Isaiah 43:4, Psalm 139, Song of Songs 4:7; 6:9, Romans 8:38–39, Jeremiah 31:3, Ephesians 3:20, Zephaniah 3:17, Song of Songs 2:10.

5   Psalm 121:4.

6   Lamentations 3:23.

7   Ephesians 3:18–19.

Chapter 5: A Father Who is Committed to Your Success

1   Philippians 1:6

2   2 Corinthians 3:18

3   Jeremiah 29:11, NIV

4   Romans 8:28

5   The Source New Testament by Dr. A. Nyland, pg. 345.

6   John 18:18

7   John 21:9

8   John 21:15-17

Chapter 6: A Lavish Father

1   Luke 15:11–32.

2   Luke 15:17.

3   Remember that it's the kindness of God that leads us to repentance (Romans 2:4).

4   Hebrews 10:17.

5   2 Corinthians 5:20.

6   Brennan Manning, *The Ragamuffin Gospel: Good News for the Bedraggled, Beat-Up, and Burnt Out* (Colorado Springs, CO: Multnomah Books, 2005), 22.

7   Robert Farrar Capon, *Between Noon and Three: A Parable of Romance, Law, and the Outrage of Grace* (San Francisco, CA: HarperCollins, 1982), 114–115.

Chapter 7: Clearing Up the Misconceptions

1   Exodus 20:18–21.

2   Exodus 34:29–35.

3   1 Samuel 8:4–8.

4   John 14:9.

5   John 5:19.

6   John 10:30.

7   James 1:17.

8   Read Galatians 3:13–29 for a greater understanding of our lineage through Jesus to receive the blessing first given to Abraham.

9   Revelation 2:4.

10   John 15:15.

11   James Hewett, *Illustrations Unlimited* (Carol Stream, IL: Tyndale House Publishers, 1988), 72–73

Chapter 8: The New Covenant of Grace—Too Good to be True?

1   Genesis 22:17.

2   You can read about the covenant with Abraham and how we are included in that covenant in Genesis 12–17 and Galatians 3.

3   Genesis 15:17.

4   Genesis 15:6 and Romans 4:3. Read the entire chapter of Romans 4 to get a much clearer picture of Abraham's faith.

5   Deuteronomy 11:26–27.

6   John 19:30.

7   Matthew 5:17.

8   Galatians 3:24.

9   Matthew 27:51.

10   Romans 6:8; Colossians 3:3; Romans 6:4; Colossians 2:12.

11   Ephesians 2:6; Colossians 2:12; 3:1.

12   Romans 8:33–34.

13   Matthew 9:1–8.

14   Matthew 9:2 NIV.

15   John 14:6 NIV.

Chapter 9: It's Time to Rest

1   Luke 18:16–17.

2   Hebrews 4:7.

3   Matthew 10:7 NCV.

4   Colossians 1:27.

5   John 6:29 NIV.

6   On August 8, 2004, Lorie was completely healed from MS. You can read her story by going to www.kingdomofgraceministries.org.

7   Revelation 12:10.

8   Colossians 2:15.

9   John 8:32.

10   John 14:26; 16:12–15.

11   Steve Schultz is the founder and chief editor of Elijah List, a prophetic e-mail publication you can receive daily by signing up at www.elijahlist.com. The full article, "God Grades on the Cross, Not on the Curve," can be found at http://www.elijahlist.com/words/display_word.html?ID=1154

12   Psalm 46:4.

13   Ezekiel 36:26.

14   John 10:27.

15   Romans 6:6.

16   Joshua 1:9.

Chapter 10: Know Your Greatness and Walk in It

1   Genesis 1:25.

2   Genesis 1:31.

3   Sandy is not her actual name.

4   Daniel 11:32 NKJV.

5   Ephesians 1:18–21.

6   Kris Vallotton, *The Supernatural Ways of Royalty* (Shippensburg, PA: Destiny Publishers, 2009).

7   Malachi 4:2.

8   1 John 4:10.

9   Romans 2:4.

10   Exodus 33:19.

11   2 Corinthians 3:13.

12   1 John 3:8.

13   Matthew 19:26.

14   Strong's Concordance 5273-hupokrites.

15 John 6:32.

16 Song of Songs 4:7.

17 Taken from truths found in Psalm 20:6; Isaiah 43:1-2; 54:17; Jeremiah 1:5; 29:11; 31:3; Malachi 3:6; Romans 8:28-39; 2 Corinthians 3:18; 12:9; Philippians 2:13; Colossians 1:27; 2:15; 1 Thessalonians 5:18.

Chapter 11: Love Is the Answer

1 Matthew 10:8 NIV.

2 Luke 9:54.

3 Read 1 Kings 18:20–40 and 2 Kings 1:9–12.

4 Romans 5:8.

5 This powerful prophetic word was spoken by Pastor Karena Lout of Blazing Fire Church in Pleasanton, CA.

6 Mark 16:17–18; Luke 4:18; 1 Corinthians 2:2–5.

Chapter 12: The Father's Blessing

1 Song of Songs 2:4.

2 Young's Literal Translation (public domain)

3 A CD soaking track of this Father's blessing can be purchased at www.brentlokkerministries.com for you to listen to over and over again as it goes deep into your heart! A link to this track on YouTube can also be found at www.brentlokkerministries.com.